ECUMENICAL THEOLOGY

Ecumenical Theology

AND THE ELUSIVENESS OF DOCTRINE

Paul Avis

First published in Great Britain 1986
SPCK
Holy Trinity Church
Marylebone Road
London NW1 4DU

British Library Cataloguing in Publication Data

Avis, Paul D.L.
    Ecumenical theology and the elusiveness of
    doctrine
    1. Ecumenical movement
    I. Title
    262'.0011   BX8.2

    ISBN 0-281-04185-7

Photoset and printed in Great Britain by
Photobooks (Bristol) Ltd.

Contents

*You cannot have Christianity
and not have differences.*

John Henry Newman

Preface

It was the publication of the Anglican-Roman Catholic International Commission's *Final Report* in 1982 that originally provoked the writing of this book. The weaknesses of that statement, seen in the light of the manifest criteria of any critical theology, provided the original stimulus. The following chapters naturally bear the marks of the critical, interrogative provenance of the book's first draft. A pilot study that appeared in *Theology* (November 1983) reflects this too in a certain abrasiveness of tone.

But obviously it is not enough to be critical and to pull down: it is necessary to be constructive and to build up. As the book developed and expanded, the constructive intention became the dominant one. The result is an attempt to specify the theological horizons of an ecumenical theology. The ARCIC documents are subjected to analysis as a foil to the developing argument. So the *Final Report* (hereinafter referred to as ARCIC) provides the point of departure, and the argument takes off from there. But it travels far afield into Reformation theology, the classical Anglican divines, Coleridge, Maurice, Newman, Gore, Temple and Ramsey, Catholic Modernism, Vatican II and the ecclesiological work of Rahner, Lonergan and Küng. It ventures into the area of theological method, with some reference to personalist philosophy, the philosophy of science and the sociology of religion. In other words, although this book engages vigorously with issues of contemporary concern - especially to the Roman Catholic and Anglican traditions - it attempts to transcend the questions of the moment and to articulate an approach to ecumenical theology that is of lasting validity.

This book differs from the ARCIC statements in tone and

method. In both it eschews the niceties and subtle obliqueness of ecumenical diplomacy.

The *method* is largely comparative and historical. I refer to the sources of our traditions. While ARCIC revealingly shuns this approach as likely to lead to deadlock (pp. 1f), I have worked on the assumption that historical sources embody the corporate memories of their churches and that any agreement that does not respect this fact will be superficial or illusory.

Writing as an Anglican, I have tried to develop what cannot avoid being a specifically Anglican response to some major problems in ecclesiology. In this, I hope I have gone some way towards meeting what seem to me to be the legitimate demands of Cardinal Ratzinger, in his article 'Anglican-Catholic Dialogue - Its Problems and Hopes' (p. 7), and of the Sacred Congregation for the Doctrine of the Faith hereinafter referred to as SCDF, in its *Observations on the Final Report of ARCIC*, that this exercise should be conducted with the requisite reference to Anglican confessional documents. To do this is of course not as simple as the apparently ingenuous request makes it sound - no doubt that is why astute Catholic defenders of the faith like Ratzinger insist that we try it!

It is possible to measure the carefully balanced phrases of ARCIC 1 against the authoritative documents of the Roman Catholic Church, using H.J.D. Denzinger's *The Sources of Catholic Dogma* or the English translation of selected doctrinal documents published recently under the provocative title *The Christian Faith* (hereinafter referred to as DC). This has been done - with depressing results - in SCDF. But it is by no means a straight-forward matter to compare them with the Anglican tradition, whose confessional documents are not so easily identifiable and have a somewhat problematic status (though not as problematic as some of the dogmatic ballast that the Roman Catholic Church has to transport with it on its pilgrimage!). Consequently, interpreters of Anglicanism are sometimes compelled to resort to an appeal to its spirit or 'ethos'. This necessity is often regarded as the Achilles heel of Anglicanism, especially by those - Anglicans or Roman Catholics as the case may be - who require a cut-and-dried propositional statement of Christian truth. But to those who hold to a 'personalist' understanding of truth as a reality that is open to discovery through praxis rather than theory, through Christian life and liturgy, it is certainly not something to be defensive about.

The weakness of contemporary Anglicanism in systematic theology – a discipline that embraces philosophical and historical theology as well as Christian doctrine – has frequently been highlighted in recent discussion. It has also been pointed out that this weakness is particularly apparent in ecclesiology. The present work – following upon *The Church in the Theology of the Reformers* (1982) which was largely historical – should be regarded as an interpretation of Anglican ecclesiology, as well as Anglican theological method generally, in the light of current questions. So although it takes its rise from controversial matters that will engage the attention of the Anglican Communion during the rest of the '80s, I hope that it has a lasting value in interpreting the Anglican tradition both to Anglicans themselves and to members of other traditions, especially Roman Catholics.

The *tone* of this book is sometimes unashamedly polemical – not in the sense of caricaturing views with which one does not agree or holding them up to ridicule or execration (in the Church of England we are familiar with these methods in the antics of extreme Protestant or Anglo-Catholic pressure groups) – but in the sense of sharpening the arguments, bringing the issues out into the open and not allowing real and serious differences between the two churches to be glossed over with a veneer of ecumenical clichés.

Some will object that I have not caught the spirit of ARCIC – that an irenic document, breathing the spirit of reconciliation, does not deserve such rough handling. It is perfectly true that there are aspects of the various statements that do not merit the sort of critical treatment that I have applied to other aspects which, in my view, do invite it. We may indeed be grateful to the commission where it has achieved genuine and solid common ground that can be recognized by the two traditions while remaining true to themselves. It has not been my intention to discuss these. But I am well aware that a new situation arises when Christians begin to talk *to* - rather than *about* - each other, and that the criticisms of people like myself who observe from the sidelines are in a sense parasitic on the valuable and strenuous efforts of those who are involved at first hand.

Furthermore, any intention to try to sabotage the movement towards unity, that seems to be gathering momentum in the Anglican and Roman Catholic churches, has been furthest from my thoughts. Those on both sides who would like to see it fail are not entitled to take comfort from these pages. But when two great Christian communions, with their enormous resources of spirituality and scholarship, devote what are presumably their best minds to intensive discussions that take twelve years to complete, we are surely justified in taking the end product as more than a bouquet of edifying sentiments. We are in fact duty-bound to examine every carefully constructed phrase, to take the argument apart at the seams, to press our questions fairly hard in an attempt to see what solid theological substance the statement will yield.

My own (tentative) belief is that there are no insuperable *doctrinal* barriers between the Anglican and Roman Catholic churches. I fully expect the second series of conversations now getting under way (ARCIC 2) to achieve substantial agreement on the really crucial issue of salvation (including justification), which will entitle us to make an impassioned and informed plea for the barriers to intercommunion to be officially dismantled - just as they are already being broken down unofficially.

That is of course not the same as saying that a full union of the two churches is even remotely attainable as things stand, or that there are no serious doctrinal differences between them. Fundamental differences there are - but the apparently *insuperable* ones are not of a doctrinal nature. They are differences of 'horizon', of ultimate assumptions regarding the approach to truth and the methods, norms and sources of theology.

This divergence of approach reflects different degrees of involvement in modern thought stemming from the Enlightenment, with its characteristic historical, relativistic, pluralistic

approach. Anglicanism, lacking a central magisterium to lay
down the limits of theological enquiry, has exercised a broad
and pervasive hospitality to these assumptions of modern
thought. Roman Catholicism, because of its disciplinary
structure, has not done so to anything like the same extent –
except in the case of individual theologians who, as a result, are
regarded as a threat. Though it is true that a movement within
Anglicanism will always be able to speak to a movement within
Roman Catholicism, there is not the *rapport* between the two
communions in their ultimate assumptions as confessing
churches to support a degree of unity that goes beyond intercommunion, with the mutual recognition of ministries, at this stage.

These ultimate assumptions concern the nature of truth, the
character and claims of reason, the status of dogmatic
statements, the meaning of revelation and the extent of
contingent human and historical elements in its interpretation
and transmission. ARCIC 1 barely touched on these. But some
will ask, What have these questions to do with learning to love
God together and worshipping and serving in one church – why
should they be a barrier? To which I reply that the practical and
pastoral implications of these deep-seated differences would
soon become apparent in a prematurely unified church, in
divergent interpretations of the scope and function of authority
in the church – blowing wide open any contrived scheme of
unity. ARCIC of course discusses the question of authority, but
my point is that it does this precisely without going into the
controversial presuppositions on which one's doctrine of
authority is constructed.

The process of liberalization and diversification needs to go
considerably further in the Roman Catholic Church, but above
all it needs to receive the recognition and blessing of the central
magisterium (and this of course would be suicidal for the
magisterium as at present constituted), before there could take
place a marriage of true minds. Vatican II reflects a tentative
attempt to come to terms with this issue. From the point of
view of the position adopted in this book, we have to think in
terms of Vatican III!

My text was completed before the publication in English of

the significant work *Diversity and Communion* (1984) by the veteran Roman Catholic theologian Yves Congar. This influential theologian of the Second Vatican Council there argues, with a weight of patristic learning and a profound insight into the Christian tradition, for a conception of Christian unity that permits considerable latitude of doctrinal positions. Congar accepts that 'diversity is an intrinsic value of unity' and concedes that there can be 'a diversity of dogmatics in the unity of faith'. He reminds a church which has tended to assume that 'all disagreement is a consequence of sin', that tensions and conflicts, openly faced, can be beneficial. In a moving personal statement, Congar confesses that all the research of his old age is directed towards the goal of unity between the Roman Catholic Church and her sister churches of East and West, based on a 'necessary but sufficient minimum of common doctrine'. *Diversity and Communion* is not primarily an investigation of what those doctrines might be, but an impressive statement of the presuppositions of such an investigation. To this extent, Congar's book serves a purpose complementary – if I may venture to say so – to my own.

In order that this dream of Christian unity might one day become a reality, I have thought it appropriate to subject these horizons of method to a fairly rigorous analysis informed by a strong constructive intention, and in so doing to attempt to lay the groundwork of an Anglican ecumenical theology – one of my assumptions being that any worthwhile theology will be ecumenical in its orientation, in the sense that it will not be satisfied with a merely domestic function.

In the first part of the book, I examine the concepts of revelation and the knowledge of God, and the doctrinal formulae in which these find interpretation, in the light of modern personalist philosophy, the philosophy of science and the sociology of knowledge. I argue that these disciplines reveal that the deepest significance of meaningful assertions about reality is located in what Michael Polanyi calls the tacit dimension of personal knowledge, and is brought to light, not by explicit discursive reasoning, but through the exercise of imaginative insight involving the whole person.

In the central section of the book, I attempt to show how these considerations, combined with the phenomenon of chronic pluralism in the churches, severely curtail the ability of the Christian community to come to a common mind on controversial issues, and the capacity of the churches' teaching authorities to formulate theological positions that will command wide agreement. I draw the conclusion – unwelcome in some quarters, I fear – that what we are trying to achieve in current ecumenical dialogue may require radical rethinking.

In the closing chapters, I go on to show that my conclusions, on the face of it so disconcerting, in fact contain the seeds of hope for an approach to Christian unity that respects both the transcendent mystery of God and the personal nature of religious affirmations.

Though wholly constructive in intention, the argument of this book frequently takes the form of demolishing pretensions, undermining common assumptions, and placing restrictions on claims that might be made. It makes a space for a degree of agnosticism in ecclesiology by compelling recognition of irreconcilable pluralism within the Church and spelling out the consequences of this for ecumenism. I recognize the critical and sometimes negative tenor of the argument. However, I do not want to leave it there. I want to go on to enquire what principles of coherence the Christian faith can offer to counterbalance a pluralism that threatens the Church with fragmentation. I want to ask whether there is a grammar of faith, a pattern of the truth, a central focus, a common foundation on which a modest ecclesiology for a pluralistic age can be built. I hope that there will be an opportunity to attempt this in the not too distant future.

I must record my thanks to Professor Louis Weil, Canon Leslie Houlden and Mrs Cynthia Shattuck, the editor of the Cowley Press, for suggested improvements, to the editorial staff of SPCK for their cordial co-operation and support and to Mrs G.M. Piper for much helpfulness with the typing.

Paul Avis
21 February 1985

Prologue

Affirming the Mystery

In common with all other intellectual disciplines - arts and sciences alike - theology sets out to explore reality. Theology is not concerned, as critics like Feuerbach, Marx and Freud would have it, with the realm of illusion, deception and wish-fulfilment, but solely with reality itself. God is, by definition, the ultimate reality, and the reality of God is the ultimate presupposition of theology, providing us, as Hans Küng puts it with 'a final point of reference, a unity, value and meaning' (1977, p. 295). The reality - or as Karl Barth preferred to say, the actuality of God - is the ultimate existential concern of all Christians, and not only of all Christians, but of all human beings. Our deepest and most passionate concern is with the question of the source of our being.

God is the all-determining reality. He is the reality that determines all reality. The world must be explained in terms of God; not God in terms of the world. The world is dependent on God; not God on the world.

But here we must pause to insert a word of qualification. In the final analysis the statement, 'The world is dependent on God, not God on the world', is theologically valid, but in its compression of truth it is unbalanced. In modern thought such influences as Hegelian immanental philosophy, process theology and simple reflection on the vast scale of human suffering have helped us to recover the authentic biblical insight that God is wholly committed to his creation, yearns for it and suffers with it. In this sense, it would be a permissible figure of speech to reverse our statement and to say that God is dependent on the world. However, other biblical and theological insights remind us that this involvement is a voluntary act of stupendous self-emptying, self-sacrifice, condescension and

1

humility on the part of the Creator-Redeemer God. It is not - as with much human love and involvement - a deficiency or incompleteness in the subject that requires completion or fulfilment from another. To affirm the self-sufficiency (aseity) of God is not the same as to deny that he can suffer (impassibility).

Every aspect of reality must be ultimately understood in the light of God's reality. No aspect of life is outside his ultimate determination. The Hebrew prophets came to understand this: the God who had brought their ancestors out of bondage, and given them a universal law to live by, could not be limited by territorial frontiers or the rival jurisdiction of other supposed gods. He who had redeemed was none other than he who had created. And so the cult of a tribal deity gave way to a universal, monotheistic religion. God was affirmed to be the all-determining reality.

The Church is always prone to diminish God: it would like a tame cultic god who remains merely a function of its liturgy. But God is not bound by rubrics; he is not trapped in our tradition; the Spirit blows where it wills. We find him when we ask, In what ways do we find reality?

God is the all-transcending reality. The Greeks had an altar 'to the unknown God'. Even to the Church God will always remain unknown. We remain mysterious to each other: how much more must God be mysterious to us. As Rahner has emphasized, in revealing himself, the hidden God becomes present 'as the abiding mystery', and that mystery, that hiddenness, will remain even in heaven (*XVI*, p. 238).

Because God is the all-transcending reality, there has stood, alongside affirmative theology, negative (apophatic) theology. Whatever we want to say about God stands in its literal sense only to be cancelled out. Our speech about God is constricted by analogy. God is love, but our most consuming experiences of love are a pale flicker compared with the great 'fire of love' that is the heart of God. God is wise, but not as we humans are wise - learning painfully, piecemeal, by trial and error, by bitter experience, by arduous study. 'The foolishness of God is wiser than [the wisdom of] men' (1 Cor. 1.25).

As *The Cloud of Unknowing* tells us: 'Of God himself can no man think. Therefore I will leave on one side everything I can think and choose for my love that thing which I cannot think. Why? Because he may well be loved but not thought. By love he can be caught but by thinking never.' Then, instructs the anonymous English mystic, 'Strike that thick cloud of unknowing with the sharp dart of longing love' (pp. 59f).

I have chosen to quote from *The Cloud* rather than from pseudo-Dionysius, Augustine or Aquinas, Luther with his hidden God, Barth in his commentary on Romans or Tillich with his concept of the God beyond God, or from writers in the Orthodox tradition. But all these writers tell us this: God is the all-transcending reality, infinitely surpassing all we think we can know or say about him.

But does not the Incarnation change this radically? 'The light of the knowledge of the glory of God' shines forth from 'the face of Christ' (2 Cor. 4.6). But this unveiling is at the same time a veiling, for God transcends even his revelation of himself. It is precisely the 'glory', i.e. the ineffable nature, of God that is revealed. As von Balthasar puts it, 'It is true that in Jesus Christ the mystery of the ground of the world burns out more brightly than anywhere else. But on the other hand, it is precisely in this light that for the first time and definitively we grasp the true incomprehensibility of God' (p. 22). The more we reflect on the holy child of Bethlehem and the suffering man of Calvary, the more we realize how little we know of God and his counsels. 'O the depth of the riches and wisdom and knowledge of God! How unsearchable are his judgements and how inscrutable his ways!' (Rom. 11.33).

What Christian doctrine tells us about God does not answer our questions in the accepted sense of that phrase. Theology is not knowledge as we understand knowledge, but, as the Christian tradition has long known, a form of learned ignorance (*docta ignorantia*). While this conclusion can be established on metaphysical, biblical or mystical grounds, we are likely to be particularly impressed today by the evidence supplied by the facts of division among Christians. As Gerald Downing has astringently remarked:

To suggest that Christians (most if not all) with their wars, arguments, schisms and heresies, their espousal of precisely opposite courses of action, in good conscience, sure they do God service, actually know him, is so monstrous an absurdity as only to persist through its enormity: it is so patently untrue, we don't know how to begin to rebut it (p. 335).

What does it imply for our understanding of revelation and attempts to put it into words, for the scope and status of doctrinal propositions, that God is the all-transcending reality?

God is the all-encompassing reality. One of the most sublime and seductive concepts of God was that of Aristotle. It is perhaps the only pure form of deism ever propounded. Aristotle postulated an unmoved mover, a self-sufficient deity, engaged in the highest of all forms of existence, pure thought or contemplation; the object of its contemplation being the highest of all possible objects, namely itself and its own perfections. But there existed - unknown to God - a world, composed of concentric spheres, which moved with a sublime desire for God.

That concept serves as a foil to the Christian doctrine of God which is, of course, not that of an unmoved mover, but of an all-encompassing reality. In the Bible, the breath of God moves upon the face of the deep (Gen. 1.2). The Lord God walks in the garden of the world (Gen. 3.8). 'Thou hast watched over me, before and behind,' the Psalmist recalls with awe, 'and hast spread thy hand over me . . . Whither shall I go then from thy Spirit, or whither shall I go from thy presence?' (Ps. 139. 5,7). 'In him we live and move and have our being,' quotes St Paul, 'He is not far from any one of us' (Acts 17.27f).

God himself inspires our search for him. But it is not the fruitless quest for someone who cannot be traced. It is a journey into a fuller personal fellowship with someone who, though present, will always remain a source of unfathomable mystery - as when blind people run their fingers over the faces and features of friends whom they will never actually see. As Christ speaks to the soul in Pascal's *Pensées*, 'You only seek me because you have already found me.'

Transcendent, unknown in his ineffable nature, dwelling in light unapproachable, yes. But in our darkness, as we 'seek God in the hope that we might feel our way towards him and find him' (Acts 17.27), a hand is in turn outstretched to us. It is the touch of a personal God and bears the print of a nail.

The struggle to affirm the supreme reality of God as the source of all and our true blessedness was reflected in the mind of one particular Christian theologian in the ancient world. The writings of Augustine (especially the *Confessions*, *The City of God* and the works against the Manichees) were an attempt to assert against the prevailing philosophies and religions the great principle that forms the presupposition of Platonic, Jewish and Christian thought, that God is the all-determining, all-transcending, all-encompassing reality. And if there is one modern theologian whose work is marked by a profound sense of the reality of God, it is Friedrich von Hügel – a Roman Catholic, suspect to his own church and an object of fascination to Anglo-Catholics. Von Hügel entitled his (incomplete and undelivered) Gifford Lectures *The Reality of God*, and his essay on 'Religion and Reality' still repays study today.

In the chapters that follow I want to ask what implications the Christian affirmation of the reality of God – all-determining, all-transcending, all-encompassing – has for the way we may speak of him in doctrines and dogmas, and what it means for the truth of God to become incarnate, so to speak, in human discourse. To begin to answer this question necessitates a change of key and our first plunge into polemics.

1

Truth and Reality

Let me begin with a topical reference. One of the least satisfactory aspects of the Anglican-Roman Catholic conversations so far, is that the discussions have apparently been confined almost entirely to purely doctrinal matters. Even the question of authority has been treated from a merely doctrinal (and to some extent, canonical) point of view. But surely, someone will reply, it is precisely in the area of doctrine that the differences lie - what else would you expect them to talk about?

My answer to that question is that I would certainly hope that substantial agreement could be reached on many aspects of Christian doctrine, but that I am not optimistic that this can be achieved on the really thorny problems until the ground has been prepared by thrashing out a common approach to the most basic assumptions of our theology. Agreement will be either unattainable or illusory unless the two parties set out from the same set of presuppositions - or at least understand clearly where they hold different ones and the theological consequences of this. Among these introductory questions of fundamental theology I would include discussion of:

(a) modern theological *method* in relation to the theological methods of the past, consciously or unconsciously employed, and to the methodologies of other disciplines;

(b) the nature of *revelation* and to what extent it may be conditioned or refracted by our human response to it;

(c) the character of *truth* in relation to personal and impersonal realities;

(d) the logical and linguistic status of *doctrines* and the role of doctrinal formulae in the Church's understanding of the truth.

We cannot be sure that these questions were not considered in depth by ARCIC 1 prior to formulating its various statements. Publication of *Anglican-Orthodox Dialogue* (1985) has made it apparent that fundamental issues of revelation, Scripture, and the knowledge of God were the subject of a number of unpublished preparatory papers in conversations with the Orthodox churches. It has to be said, however, that neither in the case of ARCIC 1 nor in that of Anglican-Orthodox dialogue, are these matters adequately reflected in the agreed statements. Are we to draw the conclusion that the most fundamental questions of Christian theology, regarding our knowledge of God in his revelation, are assumed to be uncontested and non-controversial as far as ecumenical dialogue is concerned? Ecumenical dialogue that does not take seriously such fundamental and determinative issues, but plunges straight into the thickets of doctrine, is courting accusations of dilettantism and a cavalier approach.

Questionable Assumptions

The root of the problem seems to be that the Anglican members of ARCIC have been willing to go along with a concept of truth (and error) that is deeply entrenched in the Roman Catholic tradition, but profoundly inimical to the ethos of Anglicanism. It is the difference between a *propositional* (or analytical) and a *personal* (or fiduciary) understanding of the nature of truth.

The *propositional* view pays lip-service - as all Christian theology is compelled to do - to the ineffable nature of the divine mystery. Vatican I teaches, for example, that 'divine mysteries by their very nature so excel the created intellect that, even when they have been communicated in revelation and received by faith, they remain covered by the veil of faith itself and shrouded as it were in darkness' (DC, pp. 45f). But in spite of such disclaimers, this approach assumes that truth is reducible to propositions, that it is aptly described as 'the deposit of faith', that truth and error are quantifiable entities and that you can exclude error from the Church just as you can keep draughts out of the house. It understands faith to be

7

fundamentally intellectual assent, as 'believing to be true what has been divinely revealed', or authoritatively taught. As Vatican I put it, the teachings of the Bible, tradition, and the magisterium (teaching office) 'are to be believed with divine and Catholic faith as having been divinely revealed.' Even Vatican II, which so often strikes a strongly personalist note, sometimes lapses into this vein, leaving an impression of ambivalence and of incompletely harmonized positions. Thus the Constitution *Dei Verbum* speaks splendidly of faith as that quality 'by which man freely commits his whole self to God', but then lamely adds, 'freely assenting to the revelation granted by him' (DC, pp. 557, 43, 56).

The propositionalist view goes back to Aristotelian logic and persists in all forms of scholastic theology informed by Aristotelianism. As Küng has pointed out, it received powerful reinforcement through the influence on Catholic theology of Descartes' stress on the epistemological criteria of clarity and distinctness (1971a, pp. 133ff). However, there are many Catholic theologians (especially those influenced by philosophical idealism, such as Rahner, Lonergan and Küng) who are highly critical of the propositionalist notion of truth that is characteristic of the Catholic theological tradition, and who themselves espouse a personalist view. Thus Rahner writes that the concept of truth is not purely intellectual but requires existential engagement and obedience; the Church's thinking about the central realities of its faith is like a lover articulating his love to himself; the propositions of faith are personal statements and not in the same category as the propositions of mathematics or logic (I, pp. 44f, 63ff, 68f).

A Personal Approach

The *personal* approach, by contrast, conceives of truth as apprehension of reality – a reality of which, as we have already shown, we may have a growing awareness and a real, though chronically incomplete, apprehension. A central conviction of the personal and fiduciary view (so called because it takes experience and the language that articulates it on trust as part of a given whole) is that because reality so transcends our understanding, it also defies explicit formulation.

Reality remains a mystery that does not lend itself to clear and distinct description. The closest we can come to capturing reality in words remains at the level of the tacit rather than the explicit. Our most refined and exact concepts are but blunt instruments for the delicate task of interpreting a world of meaning that in its heights and depths surpasses the furthest reach of human imagination. Myth, poetry, symbol, metaphor and analogy come closest and point us forward, triggering the leap of reason, but ultimately themselves fail. As Philip Toynbee wrote in his book of *pensées*, *Towards the Holy Spirit*, 'What lies about us is not so much the as-yet-unexplored as the inherently unexplorable' (p. 16).

The understanding of truth as apprehension of reality goes back to the beginnings of the Western intellectual tradition. In classical Greek, truth is contrasted with appearance: what is beyond appearance is truth, i.e. reality. The Hebrew of the Old Testament understands truth in terms of faithfulness, and develops what we are constrained, at the risk of anachronism, to call a 'personal' understanding of the truth of God as his faithfulness to his name and nature. As Michael Ramsey has written, for the Old Testament the truth of God is his 'saving plan as he rules in history with righteous purpose' (1936, p. 121). For the Psalmist, the truth is something that one does, follows or walks in.

In the Pauline and particularly the Johannine literature of the New Testament, a 'personalist' view of truth as divine reality is also presented. Truth comes into the world hand-in-hand with grace in the incarnation of the one who came to bear witness to the truth. To believe in him is to experience him in praxis as the way, the truth and the life. Those who receive his word belong to the truth and have it dwelling in them. As they come to know the truth they experience its liberating power. 'Truth' (*aletheia*) in the New Testament has the sense both of the Hebrew (that which is wholly reliable) and of the Greek (the real state of affairs).

Already within the New Testament, however, the concept of

truth begins to shift from its primary meaning of reality as apprehended towards the notion of authoritative teaching (the 'form of sound words': 2 Timothy 1.13), thus providing a basis for the development of the notion of dogma in which, as Bultmann says, 'truth and law are conjoined'. In dogma, as Bultmann implies, the dynamic notion of truth as a reality that we encounter, and into which we are initiated as participants, is forced into the straitjacket of propositions that in clarity and precision resemble legal formulae (pp. 232-51).

But this process marks a departure from the true spirit of the Christian faith. Christianity, as the distinguished personalist philosopher John Macmurray has written, 'is the exponent and the guardian of the personal, and the function of organized Christianity in our history has been to foster and maintain the personal life and to bear continuous witness, in symbol and doctrine, to the ultimacy of personal values' (1957, p. 30). The truth of religion is concerned with the personal disclosure of an ultimate reality that is transcendently personal and with whom we may enter into fellowship in solidarity with other persons. Doctrines are, in the final analysis, verbal crystallizations of a common experience – the received form in which relations between personal beings are expressed. To treat them as impersonal propositions, like scientific theories or codes of positive law would be not only misconceived but blasphemous.

The personalist understanding of truth as the approach to reality has its antecedents in Platonism, and has been absorbed into Anglican ways of thinking through the influence of the Cambridge Platonists, Joseph Butler, Edmund Burke, Coleridge, F.D. Maurice, William Temple and Michael Ramsey. This approach has obvious affinities with the teaching of Michael Polanyi about 'personal knowledge' and 'the tacit dimension' – which are themselves themes that figure significantly in the thought of Coleridge and Maurice. It is in keeping with this tradition that Michael Ramsey writes in *The Gospel and the Catholic Church* that the Church never fully understand the truth it proclaims. 'Dimly it understands what it teaches.' Its teaching office is a 'perilous' one since its grasp of truth is tentative, fragmentary and fragile (p. 126).

10

To talk, as the ARCIC report does, of utterances of the Church being preserved from error provided certain technical conditions are fulfilled, can only arise on the basis of a crude propositionalism. As far as the personalist is concerned, we are inescapably immersed in error; it is the condition of our being. Our best insights are simply the least misleading ones; our respect for personal relations is our surest guide. The truth is like the morning star rising into the heavens and shining into our hearts amid the surrounding darkness (cf. 2 Peter 1.19).

I shall offer more evidence later on, but perhaps I have said enough here to warrant the conclusion that Anglican members of the Commission have - to put it mildly - not done justice to their tradition. They appear to have traded in a priceless insight concerning the nature of truth as a dynamic apprehension of a personal reality, for a crude and rationalistic interpretation of truth and error that has already been abandoned by some of the best minds of the Roman Catholic Church.

In the rest of this chapter I shall be bringing forward evidence from the philosophy of knowledge (epistemology) to support my case concerning the nature of truth and our apprehension of it. I shall be attempting to establish two points. I shall be arguing, first, that all that is most significant in our experience arises from a dimension of which we are only tacitly aware; and second, that reason is the creative power that draws on that dimension, shaping it to purposeful effect. The discussion will therefore centre on the twin concepts of *tacit awareness* and *constructive reason*. This will be no mere digression. It will form the basis of my later argument - of immediate relevance to ecumenical dialogue - that Christian truth resists explicit formulation and that it is a product of human reason.

The Tacit Dimension

Rationality in its simplest form is merely a state of awareness. Let us try to capture this state in its most rudimentary stage - the moments of 'raw' or immediate experience. To do this, we have to turn to what we know, or can conjecture, of the inner world of babies and of primitive peoples

11

- and of ourselves at times of drowsiness or fatigue, in the twilight area between sleep and waking, and on the margins of consciousness at all times.

The classical description of infant consciousness is that of William James, who, as cited by Blanshard in *The Nature of Thought*, conjectures that the baby, 'assailed by eyes, ears, nose, skin and entrails at once, feels it all as one great blooming buzzing confusion' (p. 61).

Already, however - and this is the important point here - reason is engaged in the struggle to discriminate and does so progressively as the child develops. Arthur Koestler has compared the initial state of consciousness to 'a liquid, fluid universe traversed by dynamic currents, by the rhythmic rise and fall of physiological needs, causing minor storms which come and go without leaving any solid traces'. Gradually, he continues, 'the floods recede and the first islands of objective reality emerge; their contours grow firmer and sharper and are set off against the undifferentiated flux. The islands are followed by continents, the dry territories of reality are mapped out; but side by side with them the liquid world coexists, surrounding it, interpenetrating it by canals and island lakes, the relics of the erstwhile oceanic communion' (p. 292). Similarly, the experience of primitive peoples, as A.N. Whitehead envisages it, is of a world still largely undiscriminated, unanalysed, unfathomed - 'a dim background shot across by isolated vivid effects charged with emotional excitements' (1926, p. 24).

Immediate experience in this sense is not confined to babies and to primitive peoples - it belongs to us all on the periphery of consciousness. We all have experience in which, as F.H. Bradley put it, 'there is no distinction between my awareness and that of which it is aware.' And though immediate feeling, in which knowing and being are one, is transcended in rational reflection, 'it nevertheless remains throughout as the present foundation of my known world' (pp. 159f).

Basic consciousness is essentially a simple state consisting of crude sensations of pleasure and pain and lacking real perception, memory and recognition in which, as Blanshard puts it, 'there are no ideas of any kind, no images, no judgements, no desires, no anticipations, nothing that we should now call hopes or fears, no wishes or regrets, no sense of right or wrong, beautiful or ugly, true or false' (I, p. 67).

The characteristics of experience at this lowest level of awareness are primarily openness and unpredictability. Now these are not defects to be overcome; on the contrary, they contribute significantly to the achievements of reason at its higher levels. As Koestler reminds us, William James affirmed that 'Every definite image in the mind is steeped and dyed in the free water that flows round it. With it goes the sense of its relations near and remote, the dying echo of when it came to us, the dawning sense of whither it is to lead. The significance, the value of the image, is all in this halo or penumbra that surrounds and escorts it' (pp. 158f).

This is as near as we can come to the pure immediacy of awareness and remains highly conjectural; we can have no sure knowledge of the inner life of the infant or the primitive, nor can we look within ourselves without disturbing the pool of consciousness within. But, bearing these reservations in mind, there are two important conclusions that can be drawn at this stage.

First, all that is most significant in our thought and experience is derived from this vague, shadowy and indefinable area. Artistic creativity takes its rise there. As Koestler has argued in *The Act of Creation*, the creative process begins with the displacement of attention from the explicit to the implicit, to something not previously noticed, bringing to light hidden analogies, reminding us of tacit axioms and habits of thought. The temporary relinquishment of conscious controls has the effect of liberating the mind from certain constraints that are necessary to maintain the disciplined routine of thought, but tend to impede the creative leap. It is also significant that Koestler – here following Polanyi – stresses the role of modes of thought that exist on a more primitive level of mental organization.

In a closely comparable way, the process of discovery or problem-solving depends on the fluidity, openness and unpredictability of thinking below the threshold of explicit consciousness. We are looking for a solution to the problem, a conclusion to our search, an unknown factor that cannot be specified yet can be recognized when found. The paradox is resolved by the notion of tacit knowledge. Even though we have never seen the solution, we have an idea of it, just as we have the idea of a forgotten name when we say, 'It's on the tip of my tongue.'

Bernard Lonergan has made this insight central to his own theological method; his concept of the 'heuristic structure' follows the same pattern: 'Name the unknown. Work out its properties. Use the properties to direct, order, guide the inquiry' (1957, p. 44). The dimension of subsidiary awareness - or subception, rather than perception - provides these vital clues.

Constructive Reason

It is already clear that the mind is at no stage, not even the most rudimentary, a *tabula rasa*. It is never completely passive: the pattern of mere sensation is complicated by feeling and response, particularly the sense of pleasure or pain. Sensation is thus 'germinal perception'. Though passivity may be the more obvious characteristic of the mind at this elementary stage, it is never total, and diminishes as we proceed to higher levels of rationality. What is remarkable here is the mind's inherent power both to discern and to impose form, pattern, relations and analogies on the data presented by the senses. This point needs some expansion.

Perceptual form is both discerned and imposed. There is a reciprocal relation here: elements of give and take are both present. The way in which from time to time in the history of thought either the active or the passive aspects of reason have been stressed, represents a one-sided and unbalanced approach that is not true to life and experience.

The objectivist view, associated with Aquinas, Locke and Whitehead, stresses the mind's passivity, and teaches that perception lies in the assimilation of the subject to the object, as the object forces itself, so to speak, on our attention and makes its distinct impression on our minds. On the other hand, the subjectivist or Kantian view emphasizes the active role of the mind in imposing its own structure on the world. The subjective element in experience has been considerably exaggerated in the period since Kant. Subjectivism has long been dominant in epistemology, both in idealism and, later, in existentialism – though it is only more recently that the place of subjectivity in scientific procedure has really been reckoned with. A counterbalancing emphasis on the objective aspect of experience is now overdue – a willingness to recognize that, as J.E. Smith remarks, in experience 'we find something already there, we come up against something, we confront persons, objects, events, and we do so with the sense that we undergo or receive whatever it is that we meet without any sense of being responsible for having produced it' (pp. 12f).

If, however, we give due weight to both sides of the subject-object polarity of experience, allowing not only, with Kant, for the structure-forming power of the subject according to certain inherent 'categories', but also, with Whitehead, for the pressure of objectivities to shape the subject, we recognize both the openness of the world as, so to speak, it lends itself to our apprehension, and reciprocally, the way that we ourselves are open and amenable to the impressions that come to us from without.

Now we must look more closely at this basic act of interpretation by which we make sense of the world we encounter. Corresponding to the openness of experience, there is the rational process by which we respond to its complexity, unpredictability and interrelatedness. We may defer for the moment the 'technical' question as to whether this interpretation takes place by intuition or inference. The important thing at this stage is to recognize that in perception the mind is actively engaged in a process of interpretation and construction.

Kant and Coleridge held that this work of interpretation or construction was the function of imagination, leading us beyond the bare data of sensation and bridging the gap to conceptual thought. Imagination recognizes the universal

15

significance of each particular, applying concepts to things and giving meaning to the world we perceive so that 'meanings spring up round us as soon as we are conscious.' More recent philosophers, anxious to avoid any suggestion of faculty psychology, have preferred to speak of the whole mind acting in a certain way. Michael Polanyi has shown that the interpretation of phenomena, whether in simple perception or in scientific discovery, takes place by acts of personal judgement that cannot be replaced by processes of explicit reasoning. All our experience is of unities, rather than of things in isolation, and we have tacit knowledge of particulars through apprehension of the whole structures in which they subsist. 'We know more than we can tell.' Coleridge understood this when he noted that 'we may be said to comprehend what we cannot properly be said to understand.'

Constructive reason operates in the realm of tacit perception (or 'subception' as Polanyi calls it). 'The efforts of perception are evoked by the scattered features of raw experience suggesting the presence of a hidden pattern which will make sense of the experience.' Thus 'knowing is always a tension alerted by largely unspecified clues and directed by them towards a focus at which we sense the presence of a thing' (1962, p. 11).

There are close parallels to this in the thought of Lonergan: it is central to his theory of knowledge that the understanding grasps by insight the intelligible unity of apparently uncoordinated scraps of data presented in experience as it seeks a theory to account for them. Like Polanyi, Lonergan believes the structure of scientific discovery to be the same as the structure of simple perception. For both these philosophers, scientific progress depends, firstly, on belief in a hidden reality waiting to be explored in its inherent rationality and, secondly, on the mind's capacity for anticipating the approach of hidden truth.

Drawing on both empiricist (or objective) and idealist (or subjective) styles of philosophy, Newman devoted a lifetime's thinking to this problem, giving his definitive statement in the *Grammar of Assent*, a classical treatment of insight, intuition and inference. Newman's 'illative sense' – the sense of truth –

bears a strong resemblance to the concepts developed by modern philosophers in trying to explain intuition. Later followers of Newman have preferred to speak of the power of the whole mind active in the interpretation of experience, rather than of a separate inward faculty as Newman himself did in the concept of the illative sense.

In the *University Sermons* Newman describes the free-ranging versatility and flexibility of the mind. 'It is able, from small beginnings, to create to itself a world of ideas . . . One fact may suffice for a whole theory; one principle may create and sustain a system; one minute token is a clue to a large discovery.' Here Newman is, as so often, startlingly modern, and his words put one in mind of recent studies of the logic of scientific discovery, such as those of Popper, Polanyi and Koestler. Newman's description of the constructive power of reason at work merits quotation at length:

> The mind ranges to and fro and spreads out and advances forward with a quickness which has become a proverb and a subtlety and versatility which baffle investigation. It passes on from point to point, gaining one by some indication, another on a probability, then availing itself of an association, then falling back on some received law, next seizing on testimony, then committing itself to some popular impression or some inward instinct, or some obscure memory; and thus it makes progress not unlike a clamberer on a steep cliff who, by quick eye, prompt hand and firm foot, ascends how he knows not himself, by personal endowments and by practice, rather than by rule, leaving no track behind him and unable to teach another.

Reason for Newman is 'a living spontaneous energy within us' (1970, pp. 250ff).

To clarify the nature of constructive reason we must ask a further question: is this 'living spontaneous energy' through which we make the rational act of interpreting experience an energy that works by *intuition* or by *inference*?

Intuition is the direct and immediate vision of something held to be real or true. It is involved in the most elementary principles of thought, such as the law of non-contradiction, the use of analogy and the sense of probability. We 'see' that the affirmative and the negative of any proposition cannot both be true (or, at least, true in the same sense), and that is all there is to it. We 'see' an analogy and 'see' the direction in which cumulative probabilities are pointing. This 'seeing' we call intuition. Our apprehension of causality is also intuitive – as Hume might have realized when he found that there was no way of establishing the reality of causal connection by the path of discursive inferential reasoning. Even inference itself requires an act of intuition in which we jump from premises to conclusion, from ground to consequent.

So intuition is a more fundamental mode of thought than inference, though its scope is limited to the underlying principles of reason and to its role in the process of inference. It is the latter that looms largest in everyday life. For we know, says Newman, 'not by a direct and simple vision, not at a glance, but as it were, by piecemeal and accumulation, by a mental process, by going round an object, by the comparison, the combination, the mutual correction, the continual adaptation, of many partial notions, by the joint application and concentration upon it of many faculties and exercises of mind' (1915, p. 144).

Intuition is an essential component of every act of inference. All knowledge is inferential: there can be no by-passing the senses and the mind's work of interpretation and construction. But the process of inference is only made possible by the intuitive principles of causality, analogy, probability and so on.

I use the word *intuition* for the directly and immediately apprehended rational principles presupposed in all thinking and the word *insight* for those swift and subtle acts of reasoning, often loosely called intuitions, that employ subliminal or habitual inferences but that nevertheless can be distinguished from the more formal, explicit and disciplined processes of inference that are the prerogative of the trained mind.

As Newman puts it, there is, on the one hand, the initial process of reasoning for which no fixed laws can be prescribed and, on the other, the subsequent process of investigating our reasoning: unconscious and conscious reasoning, implicit reason and explicit reason. And to the latter, adds Newman, 'belong the words, science, method, development, analysis, criticism, proof, system, principles, rules, laws and others of a like nature' (1970, pp. 258ff). The explicit dimension is the tip of the iceberg: the tacit dimension is the great continuous mass that invisibly supports it.

It seems to be beyond us to give an adequate psychological explanation of how insight actually happens. The massive studies of Lonergan, Polanyi and Koestler are finally unable to provide this. In the nature of the case, the workings of insight are unobservable. As Plato writes in the Seventh Letter, 'Truth flashes upon the soul like a flame kindled by a leaping spark' (p. 136). Attempts to give a quasi-mechanical explanation such as Koestler's intersection of matrices or Poincaré's selection procedure result in a kind of epistemological reductionism. Insight can only be accounted for by postulating as characteristic of rationality a freedom, an openness, a heuristic vision whereby sensation is transcended in perception, perception in judgement, judgement in reflection and free ideas – a transcendent energy that reflects the creativity at the heart of all things.

Concepts and Clarity

We have been considering the question of how we come to know the truth. Next we must turn to the question of how we communicate what we know. In other words, what is the appropriate mode of expression for forms of reasoning that, through their openness to 'the tacit dimension', are continually enriched by the influx of fresh ideas and connections born of insight? What view of language corresponds to the view of rationality that we are advocating?

As a tissue of mutually qualifying metaphors, language mirrors the openness and interrelatedness of experience. Once again a principle of reciprocity may be discerned, for it is true both that language is shaped by the external world and that the world as we perceive it is itself shaped by the words, concepts and connections we bring to it. This principle of reciprocity has been stated by Pannenberg like this: 'Man, so to speak, spins a network of words and relations between words as the means for representing the inter-connection of diverse things in reality. He captures the diversity that initially seemed confused in the network of a symbolic world that he has created . . . The individual word itself represents a complex abundance of perceptions' (1970, p. 120).

The diversity of language, its richness of synonyms, does not merely represent 'chaos grinding itself into compatibility', but this proliferating richness of symbol, metaphor and analogy operates in the area between raw experience and explicit thought and enables us to assimilate and interpret the infinite variety of life in the world.

This is, in summary, the *fiduciary* view of language to be found in Coleridge and Newman as representatives of a distinctive tradition in English thought. Its antithesis is the naturalistic or *analytical* view to be found in a long line of philosophers including Bacon, Descartes, Hobbes, Locke, Bentham and the early Wittgenstein. Let us look more closely at these two rival traditions, beginning with the latter, the analytical view.

According to the naturalistic or *analytical* doctrine, language only reaches its full potential when metaphors are ironed out and a virtual univocity attained (supposing that were possible), so that each word can be treated as an isolated unit, a counter of meaning, and clarity itself becomes a guarantee of truth. It is an attempt to close language up, to 'desynonymize' (a word coined by Coleridge). The tendency can be seen at work in Descartes' search for clear and distinct ideas, Bacon's attempt to restrict metaphor to illustration, Hobbes' treatment of duty and inclination as synonyms and Bentham's identification of poetry with misrepresentation.

The *fiduciary* view of language, on the other hand, seeks to do justice to its inherent openness of texture, its richness of reference and its depth of meaning. As Philip Toynbee writes, the only language appropriate to the 'near inexpressible area of human experience' is 'a ghostly language; a language of hint

20

and suggestion; of echo and paradox; something much closer to the untranslatable communications of music than to the demonstrations of logic' (p. 63). Words must be taken on trust. We do not make them, we receive them as a grace. In Augustine's phrase: 'Unless you believe you will not understand.' It is not merely fortuitous that this view of language can be illustrated from the Anglican tradition.

When we use words carefully and conscientiously, we begin to feel, remarks F.D. Maurice, that we can enter into sympathy and fellowship with those who have spoken those same words centuries ago. We sense that in words are stored facts and truths that can lead us to a true understanding of the world and God. Taken on trust, they begin to put forth their 'living, germinating power'.

For Coleridge, Maurice's master, language is not composed of lifeless counters: it is a living organism mediating between the past and present experiences of a community. 'Words are not things, they are living powers, by which the things of most importance to mankind are actuated, combined and humanized' (1893, Aphorism 17). Coleridge would have agreed with Polanyi that the transmission of wisdom from one generation to another is implicit and informal. According to Coleridge and the fiduciary tradition, if we want to remain open to the richness of experience we should resist the pressure from scientific and technological usage to make meanings coalesce. In one of his notebook entries Coleridge asks 'whether or no too great definition of terms in any language may not consume too much of the vital and idea-creating force in distinct, clear, full-made images, and so prevent originality' (1895, p. 19).

The ambiguity of language is not a hindrance but a help towards greater understanding, given the complexity and elusiveness of real problems and the ineffable nature of ultimate truth. Attempts to close up the texture of language, to restrict its protean pluriformity, while they purport to serve truth, are in fact effectively filtering out certain elements of experience in the tacit dimension that may be harbouring clues to further insight.

Corresponding to the two views of language that we have

distinguished – the fiduciary and the analytical or naturalistic – are two opposed ideals of the sort of concepts we should seek to develop in constructive thinking. First of all, there is the ideal that was formulated by Descartes, promulgated by Hobbes and practised by Spinoza – that the proper tools of thought are *clear and distinct ideas*. Second, there is the alternative view, advanced in recent times by such philosophers as Whitehead, Polanyi and Popper, that we should be prepared to forgo some degree of clarity and precision for the sake of arriving at *broad illuminating generalities*. The implications of these alternative views for theology provide the theme of the next chapter.

2

Revelation and Interpretation

Cardinal Ottaviani, the last head of the Holy Office before its metamorphosis into the Sacred Congregation for the Doctrine of the Faith, is said to have remarked, P. Hebblethwaite tells us, that it was just as well for St Paul that he had not been obliged to submit his Epistles to the Holy Office for scrutiny: they would not have met 'our stern requirements of clarity and absence of ambiguity' (p. 39).

The criteria of clarity and precision remain in force in the Roman Catholic Church's understanding of its own doctrine. The declaration *Mysterium Ecclesiae* (1973) condemned the view that the Church's doctrines were indeterminate expressions of the truth, that they could only 'approximate' to reality and that the truth remained a distant goal that could not be attained by doctrinal statements. It also saw the process of greater clarification as one of the ways in which doctrine developed in the Church. In this it was echoing one strand in the teaching of Vatican II, which speaks of the Church's journey of faith taking the form of a deeper penetration by accurate insights of the faith once delivered to the saints (DC, p. 61; V2, p. 30).

Such a view of Christian doctrine clearly depends on a particular view of revelation. It presupposes that revelation is the communication of particular truths in propositional form, and that these propositions are largely immune to the relativities of culture and of changes of human understanding. The late John de Satgé states the position with a candour that would unnerve modern apologists for Roman Catholicism. 'The Catholic faith,' he says, 'is an objective and permanent body of teaching. It is authoritative because it preserves what God has made known.' 'The theological problem,' he adds, 'is

23

whether the divine message has been clearly received' (p. 89).

If this is indeed the character of revelation, it follows that Christian doctrine will be arrived at by a process of inference or deduction from the primary data of God's communication of the truth about himself. Newman claimed, in a statement of method that is as much Tractarian as Tridentine, that 'induction is the instrument of physics and deduction only is the instrument of theology.' He continued:

> There the simple question is, What is revealed? All doctrinal knowledge flows from one fountainhead. If we are able to enlarge our view and multiply our propositions it must be merely by the comparison and adjustment of existing truths; if we would solve new questions, it must be by consulting old answers . . . Revelation is all in all in doctrine; the apostles its sole depository, the inferential method its sole instrument and ecclesiastical authority its sole sanction.

Newman concludes: 'The divine voice has spoken once for all and the only question is about its meaning' (1915, p. 218).

An extreme form of this inferential and deductive method of theology is stated by the Russian Orthodox thinker A.S. Khomyakov and is worth noting for purposes of comparison. 'Investigation in the area of faith,' he asserts in an indictment of Western Christianity, 'presupposes certain basic data, moral or rational, which, for the soul, stand above all doubt.' The task of theology, he continues, 'is nothing but the process of the reasonable unveiling of these data.' 'Once admitted by an absolutely pure soul,' Khomyakov concludes, 'the least of these data would give it all the other data by virtue of an unbreakable though perhaps unrecognized sequence of deductions' (p. 57).

The Dogmatic Fallacy

When Newman wrote, this view was already under attack, but it has been slow to die. Von Hügel protested against the assumption that not only religion but theology was a divine communication – 'as though God himself communicated intrinsically adequate, mathematically precise formulations of

24

religion' (p. 60). More recently, Rahner for one has felt it necessary continually to combat the assumption that expositions of Christian doctrine must take their starting point from the formal declarations of the magisterium. Today not even the most conservative defenders of propositional revelation - Catholics or Evangelicals - would have the audacity to claim that the proper method of theology was primarily deductive - though to be consistent with their view of revelation, they probably ought to do so.

There is a basic theological principle at work in this approach. Newman called it 'the dogmatic principle' and expounded it in a rather breathless peroration to his essay *The Development of Christian Doctrine*. It consists in the conviction that there is a truth to be received, that theological error is immoral and incurs a dreadful judgement, that on the truth or error of our religious beliefs our eternal salvation depends. It holds 'that the search for truth is not the gratification of curiosity; that its attainment has nothing of the excitement of a discovery; that the mind is below truth, not above it, and is bound, not to descant upon it, but to venerate it'. It accepts with the Athanasian Creed 'that "before all things it is necessary to hold the Catholic faith"; that "he that would be saved must thus think" and not otherwise' (pp. 356f).

Newman believed this principle to be of the essence of Christianity. But, significantly, he admitted that he could not find it in Anglicanism.

In the next two sections, I propose to challenge this approach from two angles: first, on grounds of philosophical method, where I oppose Whitehead's significantly titled theory of 'the dogmatic fallacy' to Newman's *dogmatic principle*; second, on the basis of an alternative understanding of the nature of revelation and its interpretation.

Traditional Catholic theology - up to and including recent pronouncements emanating from Rome and to a certain extent the views on authority embodied in the ARCIC statements - has been bound up with a philosophical doctrine about the nature of truth and its expression in clear and distinct propositions. It is entirely appropriate, therefore, that this approach should be challenged first of all on philosophical grounds. We have laid the foundations for this in the previous chapter. And we have already noted Coleridge's suggestion that an obsession with clarity, by stereotyping images, might stifle original and creative thought. The fact that this hardly applies to Descartes, Hobbes and Spinoza, the chief architects of the mathematical ideal of language, is further evidence that their thought – whatever they may have claimed for it – is speculative, 'mystical' and permeated by insight working in the tacit dimension.

The first point that needs to be made is this: as we have already seen, discovery and problem-solving are only possible because all knowledge is tacit before it becomes explicit. What we know contains intimations of what we may yet discover. It is leading us to fresh approaches and new insights. As John Macmurray has astutely remarked, knowledge is not the result of thinking, but thinking presupposes knowledge, since 'we can only think about what we already know' (1957, p. 101). Though our knowledge is primarily tacit, it is enough, not only to formulate a given problem, but also to suggest its solution. But if, on the other hand, all knowledge were explicit and capable of being clearly stated, there would be no room for either problems or discoveries.

It is precisely here that we come to the parting of the ways in theology. For traditional Catholic theology (as also for pre-Enlightenment Protestant theology) the truth has been communicated 'ready made', and all we have to do is to make sure that we understand it correctly. In this we have the infallible guidance of the Church (for Protestants, the 'perspicuity of Scripture'). Any notion of discovering the truth or creatively reinterpreting the data would be completely beside the point. Hence Newman's insistence that curiosity cannot be our motive and that our attainment of truth has nothing of the excitement of discovery about it. From the point of view of the understanding of revelation being put forward in this book, however, the ideas of research, discovery and exploration are entirely appropriate.

Second, the more precise and formalized statements become,

the less they tell us. Hence Polanyi's slogan, 'We know more than we can tell.' In the social sciences and history, for example, the personal factor is prominent; interpretation is crucial. At the same time, these disciplines are rich in factual content. When we move up the scale of increased formalism, however, through the exact to the deductive sciences, the personal factor diminishes steadily and so too does the informativeness of scientific statements. As Michael Polanyi puts it: 'It is a sequence of increasing formalization and symbolic manipulation, combined with decreasing contact with experience. Higher degrees of formalization make the statements of science more precise, its inferences more impersonal and correspondingly more "reversible"; but every step towards this ideal is achieved by a progressive sacrifice of content' (1958, p. 86). The conclusion – whose application to theology is obvious – is that, in order to describe reality more fully, language must be correspondingly less precise.

Third, there is a word of caution to be spoken about careless use of the word *precise* in this context. Precision cannot be predicated of statements as such but only of statements that refer to an objective state of affairs. Purely *a priori* statements cannot be precise. As Polanyi points out, the term 'precision' can only be applied to a map or a measured quantity – namely, only in so far as the statement seems to correspond to or match reality. In other words, Descartes' ideas may have been clear and distinct, but they could not have been precise.

Let me put this from another angle. Questions of meaning must be subservient to questions of fact and truth. Provided that our terms serve their purpose, we may leave them alone and get on with the real task, which is to strive for true theories in an effort to solve genuine problems. In this connection, Karl Popper has made a sustained polemic against the obsession with defining terms and 'What is?' questions – what Popper calls 'essentialism'. 'It is always undesirable to make an effort to increase precision for its own sake – especially linguistic precision – since this usually leads to lack of clarity,' he claims. 'One should never try to be more precise than the problem situation demands . . . An increase in precision or exactness

27

has only a pragmatic value as a means to some definite end.' Popper puts this in slogan form as 'We never know what we are talking about.' Every statement has a conceptual hinterland. There is 'an infinity of unforeseeable non-trivial statements belonging to the informative content of any theory' (1976, p. 24). Over-refining of terms may bestow a spurious clarity and precision, but – as Coleridge suggests – it pares away layers of suggestiveness and informative content.

Whitehead similarly argues that for every statement 'there is always a background of presupposition which defies analysis by reason of its infinitude' (1941, p. 699). We should not, therefore, be looking for smaller and smaller units of meaning, ideas which are ever more clear and precise. Instead, we should be looking outwards – exploring the far reaches of connection, reference and context. Whitehead reminds us that our ideas are 'ignorantly entertained'; we are unaware of the 'infinitude of circumstances' to which they are relevant. Philosophical method, therefore, is 'a resolute attempt to enlarge the understanding of the scope of application of every notion which enters into our current thought' (1938a, pp. 233f). Clear and distinct ideas are a cul-de-sac: it is the broad generalizations born of insight that open the wide horizons.

We are restricted to working with generalities by the limitations of our minds – we cannot keep the whole evidence before us 'except under the guise of doctrines which are incompletely harmonized. We cannot think in terms of an indefinite multiplicity of detail; our evidence can acquire its proper importance only if it comes before us marshalled by general ideas.' These ideas are borrowed from the philosophical and cultural tradition and are for ever in a state of flux and transformation, 'either fading into meaningless formulae or gaining power by the new lights thrown by a more delicate apprehension'. Snatched perhaps from primitive, obscure or earthy contexts and pressed into the service of metaphysics in an attempt to sound the depths of reality, words and phrases are stretched to the limit and there they are stranded, 'metaphors mutely appealing for an imaginative leap' (1938b, p. 217).

Whitehead's concept of the dogmatic fallacy is a sharp attack on the proponents of clear and distinct ideas as the philosophical ideal. The fallacy lies in the assumption that 'we are capable of producing notions which are adequately defined in respect to the complexity of relationship required for their illustration in the real world'. Except for the simpler notions of arithmetic, even our more familiar ideas, apparently obvious, are infected with an 'incurable vagueness'. Clarity can only be achieved by the radical abstraction of an idea from its environment. Though this may be necessary, there is a price to be paid, and it consists in an inevitable distortion of the truth.

'Not of Words'

'Revelation is not of words,' wrote Newman on the fly-leaf of a copy of his *Development of Christian Doctrine*. Newman has come before us as an exponent of the dogmatic principle and of the propositional approach to revelation, but he is too great a thinker to be entirely reducible to the narrow defensiveness that this involves. If this were all he stood for, Newman would not have had the significance that he did have for the Roman Catholic Modernists - with their personal understanding of revelation - or for the Second Vatican Council. Thus, we find him writing in 1867 to Pusey, who wanted a clear and definitive statement of the articles of faith that were binding on Catholics and a guarantee that they would not be added to, that this would be to treat revelation as a series of propositions. 'We must ever hold, on the contrary,' Newman insisted, 'that the object of faith is not simply certain articles, A.B.C.D., contained in dumb documents, but the whole living word of God, explicit or implicit, as dispensed by his living Church' (1968, p. 79).

Through most of its history the Church has certainly believed itself to be the guardian of a body of guaranteed truth in the form of propositions, communicated to us by divine revelation, dovetailing into a coherent system of belief, and handed down as the deposit of faith that must be preserved, defended and if necessary enforced. The last vestiges of this approach remain in the belief, accepted by Congar, Rahner and

Chirico, for example, that there are indeed infallible propositions. But the tenability of such a view has been undermined by profound changes in our understanding of revelation. Newman's comment, 'Revelation is not of words,' is symptomatic of this.

Critical study of the Bible has played its part in discrediting the notion of divine truth communicated ready made, as has historical reconstruction of the development of doctrine in the early centuries of the Christian era. We learn that statements of belief were the product of reflection, recension, controversy, personal feuds, political pressure and so on. While this in itself does not detract from the truth of the Christian faith – that would be to fall into the genetic fallacy of judging truth purely by its origin – it does make it impossible to believe in a sudden burst of revelation from heaven that settled the form of the Christian faith once and for all.

Revelation cannot be isolated – except purely conceptually and schematically – from the human process of interpretation.

First, it is not isolable as to its *source*, because once a truth has been absorbed into our general outlook, its origin is irrelevant. For example, once it was necessary for it to be revealed that God is one, but now we cannot entertain any other idea of God and no one is tempted by polytheism. The truth of the unity of God has passed from the sphere of revelation into that of natural theology.

Second, revelation is not isolable as to the *mode* in which we come to know its truth. Theology is faith seeking understanding of a reality that is given – the totality of our significant experience in natural theology; the special occasions of divine disclosure in the personal mode, supremely in Jesus Christ, in theology of revelation (never 'revealed theology'). In faith's search for understanding, the mode of enquiry is the same as for all areas of research, however remote from the religious sphere. Always there is something given ('the revelational factor in all knowledge') and something discovered. As the religious philosopher W.G. de Burgh put it, 'All discovery implies revelation and all revelation implies discovery; the terms are correlative and the distinction between them, though

30

real, is one of emphasis on the subjective and the objective moments in all knowledge' (p. 108).

Third, revelation cannot be isolated from the process of human interpretation as far as its *content* is concerned. This is not controversial: Aquinas himself did not differentiate natural from revealed theology on grounds of content: revelation delivered to us the saving truths that we were generally too simple to think out for ourselves, though in principle they were attainable by unaided human reason.

Doctrines such as the Incarnation and the Holy Trinity might seem to discredit this view, since without revelation no one could be expected to arrive at these mysteries simply by reflection. But it is precisely here that the element of human interpretation is most pronounced. These doctrines are con-spicuous examples of theological construction, since they are not found in explicit form in the New Testament.

But perhaps the most effective influence in bringing about the abandonment of the propositionalist view of revelation, has been the deep transformation of the climate of thought. Personalist philosophies, percolating through into general culture during the last half-century, have undermined the conceptions of divine action and human response on which the propositionalist view is based. It no longer seems appropriate or right to think in these terms.

Instead we have come to accept an idea of revelation in which God discloses, not a set of truths, but his divine presence within human experience; not by-passing our seeking and questioning but precisely giving himself in divine condescension to be known in and through our fallible apprehension of reality. He has chosen to submit his self-disclosure to the process of refraction and distortion that is inevitable when that truth is appropriated into our thought-forms and traditions that are specific to a certain culture and stage of human understanding.

This is a view of revelation that is deeply embedded in modern Anglican thought; it is also characteristic of the ill-fated Modernist movement in the Roman Catholic Church at the turn of the century.

To take the Modernists briefly first: von Hügel gives a superb statement of the meaning of revelation as our 'deepest experience of the ultimate Reality through the action of that Reality itself' (p. 60).

George Tyrrell similarly stresses the role of creative interpretation in responding to divine self-disclosure. He lays down the thesis that 'the leading ideas of Catholic dogma . . . have been more or less consciously divined by the inventive faculty, inspired by the Spirit of Christian love'. The doctrinal, dogmatic system of Christianity, he asserts, is 'fabricated by the public Christian understanding inspired by the Spirit of Christ' (pp. 146, 139).

The voice of Roman Catholic Modernism was silenced by the two papal edicts of 1907, *Lamentabili* and *Pascendi* and it must be admitted that ecumenism is not likely to be advanced by demonstrating common ground between mainstream Anglicanism and a suppressed heresy of Roman Catholicism – though it may be that the unfortunate Modernists are due to enjoy a degree of rehabilitation after being under a cloud for so long. What cannot be gainsaid is that they echo an aspect of Anglican theology that goes back at least as far as Coleridge and has become intensified in the period since Modernism.

Newman, as we have seen, deplored the fact that his dogmatic principle was conspicuously absent from nineteenth-century Anglicanism. He will not concede that the attainment of truth has anything of the excitement of discovery. In explicit contrast we find F.D. Maurice claiming that 'discovery and revelation are . . . more nearly synonymous words than any which we can find in our language' and the Cambridge theologian F.J.A. Hort remarking that 'truth of discovery is received by everyone except the discoverer as much from without as if it were revealed,' while 'truth of revelation remains inert till it has been appropriated by a human working of recognition which it is hard to distinguish from that of discovery' (p. 75).

In a notable work, *Belief and Practice*, Sir Will Spens, the leading Anglican Modernist, set out a view of revelation and its interpretation in doctrine that in its emphasis on the notions of reality, relativism, praxis and hypothesis is strikingly modern.

Spens rejected the concept of Christian belief as 'a hard-drawn system of thought', preferring to describe it as 'an imperfect but real insight . . . an imperfect but growing knowledge of God . . . an imperfect but substantial grasp of the possibilities of experience.' The sources of theology were therefore not doctrinal propositions but the primary experiences of revelation that they presuppose. Theology should begin with the recognized facts of Christian experience and ask what hypotheses are necessary to explain them. The creeds should be taken as an expression of the experience of the early Church; it follows that we would not express our own experience of God in Christ in the same way today (pp. 3, 7f).

The propositional view of revelation received the *coup de grâce* as far as officially sponsored Anglican theology is concerned in Archbishop William Temple's celebrated dictum, 'There are no revealed truths; only truths of revelation.'

The Church of England's Doctrine Commission's report *Christian Believing* (1976) contains a valuable account by the late Geoffrey Lampe of the changes that have taken place in our understanding of revelation. Theological propositions and systems of belief, he claims, are not revealed. 'Theology is a process of reflection on faith that arises from revelatory experience; it is not itself the locus of revelation.' The great credal statements of orthodoxy, Lampe continues, 'are not timeless expressions of truth communicated from heaven, but human attempts to analyse and describe inferences drawn from men's experience of encounter with God.' We can illustrate the consequences of this for our understanding of the status of the central dogmas of Christianity from the doctrine of the Trinity as expressed in the Christian creeds. 'That God is one substance in three persons,' argues Lampe, 'is an hypothesis or model, valuable in so far as, and for so long as, it serves to give an intellectually satisfactory account of the data afforded by revelatory experience, and to articulate and explain the attitudes of faith which are grounded in that experience.' While 'it may indeed be so valuable as to be indispensable for this purpose . . . it is a human theological construction and might in principle prove to have outlived its usefulness' (pp. 102f). To

33

appreciate Lampe's point, we do not need to subscribe to his conclusion that it has indeed outlived its usefulness!

If we set alongside this exemplarily clear passage from a recent publication of the Church of England's Doctrine Commission, the equally unambiguous statement of the Declaration *Mysterium Ecclesiae*, rejecting the notion that dogmas are human constructions and asserting that all dogmas are divinely revealed (DC, p. 249), we see the extent of the discrepancy between two traditions, their respective approaches to Christian doctrine and the range of opinion that they can accommodate.

Two conclusions follow. First, the degree of doctrinal agreement already attained in Anglican–Roman Catholic dialogue should be appraised with a high degree of realism, bearing in mind that it may well conceal deep-rooted divergencies in the two churches' approach to Christian truth. Second, the same realism needs to be brought to our expectations of realizing unity. The conclusion seems to be inescapable that the process of theological freedom and liberalization within the Roman Catholic Church needs to go very much further, and to include not only eminent theologians such as Rahner but also the magisterium itself, before there can be a true and genuine meeting of minds on issues so fundamental to Christian theology as the nature of revelation and the reformability of doctrine.

An Integrated View

More than half a century ago, an Archbishop of York gave the prestigious Gifford Lectures on natural theology. (It gives food for thought that the Church of England once had an archbishop capable of doing so and that it was so long ago.) In these celebrated published lectures, *Nature, Man and God*, William Temple claimed that the traditional separation of natural theology and Christian doctrine (sometimes loosely called 'revealed theology') had been detrimental to both and could not be sustained.

If, on the one hand, he argued, natural theology is confined to the study of what has never been part of a supposed revelation, then it has to be said that 'it is concerned with what is very unimportant alike to its own students and to all mankind.' But, on the other hand, as long as natural theology – autonomous theological enquiry – claimed a monopoly of rationality, 'revealed theology' was made to look narrow, defensive and irrational. The combination of these two assumptions resulted, Temple alleged, in a situation where 'the method which had some promise of cogency could only achieve what had little interest, while all that gives interest and power to religion has its source in spheres that are not open to criticism and are therefore ignored or reverenced with equal intellectual right.' On this reckoning, Temple concluded, religion must appear 'either insecure or uninteresting' (pp. 9, 15).

However, the distinction between natural and 'revealed' theology is much too deeply ingrained in traditional theological habits to be discarded. In fact it reflects the fundamental grammar of the faith expressed in the polarities of nature and grace, reason and revelation, immanence and transcendence. Accordingly, William Temple redefined the distinction as one between methods of approach rather than spheres of interest, procedure rather than content. The method of natural theology is purely one of *rational criticism* and there is no aspect of human experience – not even revelation itself – that is exempt from rational scrutiny. So for this exponent of Anglican theology, natural theology must be taken to the heart of Christian doctrine ('revealed' theology) in the form of a rational and critical approach to religious beliefs and practices and to all the questions of theology (p. 7). Temple is advocating an integrated view of revelation and interpretation.

Temple, who had been profoundly influenced by his early study of Thomas Aquinas, was here reformulating a fundamental Thomist principle that the philosophical and theological disciplines differ in approach and method rather than in field of enquiry and content. Aquinas wrote: 'The diversification of the sciences is brought about by the diversity of aspects under which things can be known . . . Accordingly there is nothing to stop the same things from being treated by the philosophical sciences when they can be looked at in the light of natural reason and by another science [i.e. theology] when they are looked at in the light of divine revelation' (Ia, i, 1). But Aquinas's view of revelation and reason cannot be transposed directly into contemporary theology, since it depends on an understanding of revelation as given in propositions that are offered for our assent.

A position with striking similarities, but in a contemporary idiom, has been developed by Pannenberg. For him, Christian theology is not distinguished from other disciplines on grounds of content, but solely by virtue of its unique point of view: everything is to be evaluated in relation to God, *sub ratione Dei*. The central concern of theology is with the validity of claims about the reality of God. This means that the question of *revelation* must be tackled with the tools of *reason*. Theology's task, Pannenberg claims, 'is to examine the validity of the thesis of faith as a hypothesis.' To do this, it must take the whole of created reality into view. As Pannenberg puts it, 'The investigation of God as the all-determining reality involves all reality.' The task of theology is therefore the critical evaluation (reason) of religious traditions in the light of their distinctive claims (revelation) (1976, pp. 296ff, 315).

Similarly, Bernard Lonergan has deplored the separation of natural theology ('philosophy of God') and Christian doctrine ('systematics') and called for their integration along the lines indicated by Aquinas. The question of God, Lonergan asserts in *Philosophy of God and Theology*, arises through all our significant experience. In the overall enquiry concerning the reality of God, philosophical and theological elements fuse together and can only be distinguished by a conscious effort of conceptual abstraction (p. 34). In this work, and more comprehensively in *Method in Theology*, Lonergan has provided an agenda for a unified philosophical-theological discipline. He lends his support to our argument for an integrated approach to revelation and its interpretation.

Natural theology arising from rational reflection on the whole of our significant experience, and theology of revelation arising from rational reflection on the significance of those events regarded as revelatory within the totality of human history, are two interdependent aspects of one integrated theological enterprise. The distinction is conceptual, not actual. Natural theology, dealing with the whole of our significant experience, cannot hope to reach conclusions remotely adequate to the nature of reality if it leaves out of account the moments of divine disclosure and human insight that we are compelled to call revelatory. Theology of revelation, on the other hand, will be denied the understanding it seeks of the events of revelation if it abstracts them from their living context in the stream of history and the welter of human experience.

In conclusion, I want to return to William Temple. It is a remarkable fact that more than half a century ago this Anglican philosophical theologian detected the incipient breakdown of the dualism of natural and revealed theology and began to point towards a position that has been developed and vindicated by such modern theologians as Rahner, Lonergan and Pannenberg. But Temple's argument does not press the question quite far enough and seems to issue in a fallacy.

If the method of natural theology is rational and critical, that of 'revealed' theology, Temple seems to assume, is based on the acceptance of authority.

But it is only possible to hold this view where revelation is understood in a strictly propositional sense – as the communication of ready-made divine truths for our assent. Now Temple was actually a notable critic of the propositional view of revelation and we have already mentioned his saying, 'There are no revealed truths, only truths of revelation.'

The inconsistency apparent here in Temple's position seems to have arisen from a confusion of theology with religion. Temple has slipped into comparing *natural theology* with *revealed religion*: but they are not commensurate.

The practice of religion, as he rightly points out, depends for all of us up to a point, and for many people almost entirely, on acceptance of beliefs and codes of practice authoritatively delivered and devoutly accepted. But this is not the case in theology. Theology of revelation is concerned to understand an event or experience that is regarded as revelatory of God. This event or experience may loosely be described as authoritative in that it makes a claim on our attention and demands a response. But in seeking to give an ordered, informed and rational account of it theologians do not proceed on the basis of authoritative doctrines.

Even Karl Barth's concept of dogmatics as exploration of the content and significance of the *dogmata*, the doctrines of the Christian Church, in which the articles of the creed, etc., are taken as unquestionably given, did not inhibit him from being critical and even revolutionary in his treatment of the material. The only exception to this general rule would be where the Church's tradition, the decisions of councils or popes, were regarded as infallible or at least strictly binding. But then what is delivered in revelation would be prevented from exercising any critical function with regard to the tradition. This would result in a concept of revelation that was evacuated of all meaning and a notion of theology as purely deductive and self-perpetuating.

The inescapable conclusion is that the rational and critical method, the method of conjecture and refutation, of question and counter-question, of intellectual enquiry employing all the resources at our disposal, belongs not only to natural theology but also to theology of revelation. This conclusion of course merely substantiates a position that we have already reached on other grounds. For Anglicans, it has its classical mandate in the famous words of Bishop Butler: 'Reason . . . is indeed the only faculty we have wherewith to judge concerning anything, even revelation itself.' (p. 219). Reason is our interpreter; through it we explore the reality of what is given, of revelation. It is all we have and all we need, bringing with it not only logical clarity and sequential argument but also insight and imagination, moral depth and aesthetic appreciation.

Theory and Praxis

In distinguishing between a *propositionalist* and a *personalist* understanding of the nature of truth, I do not want to be understood to be advocating the completely untenable view that propositions have no part to play in our apprehension of the truth. This book consists of propositions. Christian doctrine is expressed in them. No human discourse can take place without them. My fundamental point is that propositions are not themselves 'the truth' but only derivative of the truth. As St Thomas Aquinas teaches us, truth consists in the matching of reality and mind (Ia, 21, 2c). Truth is thus an *event*. In theology it consists in the first-hand (though mediated) experience or encounter with divine reality that is granted to certain elect mystical or prophetic souls. This experience, that we rightly call revelatory, may be crystallized in propositions and so become publicly available, thereby offering the rest of us an opportunity of participating in the same gracious reality through our own comparatively impoverished experience. But until we do, we possess merely a second-hand acquaintance with the truth through the agency of propositions.

Christian doctrines consist of propositions. These have a two-fold reference: firstly to the truth that they seek to express; secondly to the persons who define, discuss and believe them. As far as their relation to the persons who hold them is concerned, there is an important distinction to be observed between personal and impersonal ways of defining doctrine in propositional form. The impersonal mode attempts a spurious objectivity; the personal mode reflects a proper involvement.

To take an example from a central area of Christian doctrine: it is true (granted the limitations of human understanding and language) to say, 'God is three persons in one nature.' That statement has an admirable objectivity but it is totally impersonal. It is not the authentic voice of Christian theology. Theology is essentially a confession of faith, even when the highest standards of scholarship and correctness are being upheld. Theological statements, wherein doctrine is articulated, are inescapably existential. We have no wish to know, and cannot even take cognizance of, what has no bearing upon our lives. The authentic voice of Christian doctrine says, not, 'God is three persons in one nature' but, 'We believe in one God, the Father, the almighty, maker of heaven and earth, of all things visible and invisible and in one Lord Jesus Christ, the only-begotten Son of God . . . and in the Holy Spirit, the Lord, the giver of life . . .'.

Clarity, precision, distinctness, objectivity are spurious when applied to statements of doctrine, since these are distillations of Christian experience – of the personal apprehension of God's truth and reality revealed supremely in Jesus Christ – and the personal dimension is not amenable to impersonal description without radical distortion taking place.

This is surely one of the valuable insights that the current obsession of theologians with practice, to the disparagement of theory, attempts to express. It begins with the recognition that the propositions of Christian orthodoxy embody not only descriptions of Christian truth, but also various ideological commitments of the Church, its leaders and individual members, to the social structure of the time. They are not pure and unadulterated statements of theory, but incorporate a praxis that may be good or bad, constructive or destructive, liberating or enslaving.

Where there is little awareness that the doctrines under consideration are not merely extrapolations from revelation, but bear all the marks of social, political and cultural influences, serve a social, political or cultural function and are defensive for some and repressive for others, there is an air of unreality and illusion about the ecumenical exercise of comparing doctrinal notes in order to reach a common position. Doctrine and tradition cannot be taken at face value, as ARCIC and, even more complacently, the Anglican-Orthodox conversations do. Their interpretation demands not only theological erudition and spiritual insight, but an acute sociological perception too.

As Charles Davis puts it: 'The body of teaching constituting tradition cannot be disengaged from the changing reality of social practice . . . traditional symbols and doctrines are part of social history, constituting the conscious component of a particular social practice.' Because theory and practice are dialectically related in this way, Davis continues, 'there is no purely theoretical centre of reference for the truth and continuing identity of tradition.' He concludes that, since the identity and truth of a tradition cannot be established theoretically, 'the religious structure we refer to as orthodoxy is rendered impossible' (pp. 8f).

I conclude that there will no longer be a single invariant doctrinal standard to which all exercises in Christian doctrine have to conform. This certainly has consequences for the notion of the magisterium put forward in the ARCIC *Final Report*. But it does not mean that there is no place for Christian theories (i.e. doctrines expressed in propositions), provided these are acknowledged to be personal, existential statements, related to praxis.

The personalist philosopher John Macmurray has reminded us that while all thought is by definition theoretical, we are called upon to think from the standpoint of action. It is life, action, that is 'primary and concrete'; thought, on the other hand, is 'secondary, abstract and derivative'. All theory arises from practical problems. This fact does not, however, entail the control of theory by practice, as some political theologians would have us accept, but rather the control of practice by theory - 'the determination, through reflection, of the ends of action' (1957, pp. 21ff, 85ff). There is no escape from theory, but its connection with praxis needs to be recognized. We cannot dispense with propositions though they must respect the intrinsic existential reference of doctrines. Their place in theology might be indicated along the following lines.

Theory and praxis are related dialectically. As we have already seen in our discussion of perception, there are, strictly speaking, no brute facts. All we encounter is already shaped by interpretation. We impose a theory on the world of raw experience, both our own and that of our remote evolutionary ancestors. This principle of reciprocity can be extended beyond the realm of individual acts of perception to cover the whole domain of natural knowledge. At all levels, fact is the product of theory; theory and praxis act reciprocally, dialectically. In theology, doctrines both embody social realities and act critically upon them.

Theory plays a vital role in method. In scientific method a hypothesis has to be formulated before it can be confirmed or

41

refuted. The theory prescribes the method of enquiry; as Whitehead points out, you cannot prove a theory by evidence that the theory itself dismisses as irrelevant. A theory also acts as a principle of selectivity – we cannot keep all the evidence before our minds the whole time (1942, p. 256). As Einstein remarked, 'A theory may be confirmed by experience: but there is no bridge leading from experience to the creation of a theory.' In physics, the role of theory has become clearer now that the questions that concern physicists have passed beyond the horizon of observability. Quantum theory represents the frontier of observation physics and relativity theory constitutes the triumph of pure theory in a realm where observation and induction are not applicable.

Applying this to theology, it follows that doctrines, as they are delivered to us by the tradition of the Church, are not a point of arrival where we halt, sit down and contemplate the view, so much as a point of departure from which we set off in exploration of a transcendent reality that remains almost wholly unfathomed.

Theories exist to solve problems. All knowledge begins, not with dispassionate clinical observations, but with problems that bother us. And problems generate in our minds theories of how to solve them. The view of knowledge as essentially problem-solving was put forward by the Pragmatists at the turn of the century and has been sponsored by Polanyi and Popper among philosophers of science, and the Catholic Modernists and Lonergan among theologians.

As Popper himself develops the idea, problem-solving applies at all levels of life on the evolutionary scale. All organisms are constantly engaged in attempting to solve the problems presented by their environment. 'The tentative solutions which animals and plants incorporate into their anatomy and their behaviour are biological analogues of theories.' The first problems and the first tentative theoretical solutions must have developed simultaneously, for 'organic structures are theory-incorporating as well as problem-solving structures' (1972, pp. 242n, 145; 1976, p. 133).

Speaking theologically then, we can say that, if all knowledge is problem-solving, and if Christian theology is concerned with the knowledge of God, it follows that it is entirely appropriate to think of God as our 'problem'. If he were not a problem to us he could not be known. As Pannenberg has expounded in his *Theology and the Philosophy of Science*, the Christian doctrines, derived from revelation, are the hypotheses by means of which the problem of God is explored and, to some extent, answers formulated.

Theories are reformable. They exist to be tested and improved. Knowledge is advanced by a process of dogmatic and critical thinking – what Popper calls 'conjecture and refutation'. A rather more speculative version of this is advocated by Whitehead: the philosopher first of all devises ideas of wide generality; he then attempts to perfect their logical coherence, modifying his theory accordingly.

Whitehead appears to play down the necessity of rigorously testing theories against the 'facts' in the way that Popper advocates. But logical refinement of a set of ideas, however perfectionist, is no substitute for submitting it to the test of experience or experiment. This presupposes that scientific theories are tentative, provisional and perfectible (1967, p. x).

In theology, similarly, while a wide range of open, speculative concepts borrowed from the common pool of philosophical ideas, will be used to formulate the theories (i.e. doctrinal propositions) of theology, these will remain provisional, tentative and reformable. The Church must have the liberty to discard theories that have lost their usefulness or proved misleading. It must be able to bury its dead. And just as scientific theories must be tested against the evidence and not allowed to run riot, so too theology demands an empirical earthing for its statements, however transcendent their ultimate reference. They must be congruent with the whole of our knowledge and integrated with the requirements of Christian practice. The Church's apprehension of truth is given, not through steadily more precise and accurate interpretations of its doctrinal formulae, but through its life of worship, prayer, fellowship, service and suffering.

3

Adequacy and Error

Compared with some other ecumenical statements, such as the Lutheran-Roman Catholic discussions in America, the ARCIC reports are notable for maximizing the area covered by the agreed statement and minimizing the areas reserved for separate confessional positions. Where the question of the inerrancy of the Church and its magisterium is concerned, the result is rather extraordinary.

The *Final Report* accepts that certain teachings and decisions of the Pope in a united church would be preserved from error (i.e. would be infallible - though the word is avoided). It is difficult to see how the Anglican members of the commission ever allowed themselves to get into the position of sponsoring this view.

The Roman Catholic Church teaches, as everyone knows, that, provided the right conditions are fulfilled, certain pronouncements of the Church's teaching authority (the magisterium: supremely, of course, the Pope) are infallible. The Anglican Church, as everyone knows, makes no such claim for itself. Are we then meant to conclude from the agreed statement that the Anglican Church should now recognize that the pronouncements of the Roman Catholic magisterium have been infallible in the past (what would this imply about polemical pronouncements such as the condemnation of Anglican orders in *Apostolicae Curae*?) and are infallible now? Does it follow that this infallibility is a charisma in which the Anglican Church can now participate for the first time by virtue of a union with the Roman Catholic Church?

It is futile to try to graft any notion of infallibility or inerrancy on to Anglicanism. But what Anglicanism is receptive to is a concept of *adequacy*. Since this distinction is also to be found in Roman Catholic ecclesiology, let me begin by illustrating the contrast between inerrancy and adequacy from the Roman Catholic situation before bringing Anglicanism into the picture.

Adequacy or Inerrancy?

As recently as 1973, the Sacred Congregation for the Doctrine of the Faith confirmed the Catholic position that it is not consistent with the church's divinely instituted teaching authority to admit an element of error in its definitive pronouncements. The Declaration *Mysterium Ecclesiae* laid it down that 'the faithful are in no way permitted to see in the church merely a fundamental permanence in truth which, as some assert, could be reconciled with errors contained here and there in the propositions that the church's magisterium teaches to be held irrevocably' (DC, p. 248). This statement reveals that a concept of truth and error as quantifiable, identifiable and isolable is still being employed.

An alternative understanding of truth as personal knowledge, adequate to a given purpose, is clearly present in Hans Küng's remarks that all human statements 'always fall short of reality, are always liable to be misunderstood, are not always translatable, are constantly on the move, shifting and changing their meaning, are so susceptible to ideology and never absolutely clarifiable.' In other words, he continues, 'they are subject to ambiguity, distortion, misunderstanding and error' (1971a, p. 139). But for Küng, as he has shown in *The Church - Maintained in Truth*, these facts neither contradict Christ's promises to his Church, detracting from the indefectibility of the Church as it continues in the truth, nor undermine the effectiveness of its teaching ministry. We may not have *inerrancy*, but what we do have is *adequacy*.

Needless to say, Christian doctrines can never be adequate to the reality that they attempt to express. Their divine object remains wrapped in impenetrable mystery, 'dwelling in light unapproachable' (1 Tim. 6.16). All Christian traditions are agreed on this. It is common to the apophatic theology of

Eastern Christianity, *The Cloud of Unknowing* tradition of English mysticism and the formulations of Catholic scholasticism. As the First Vatican Council put it: 'Divine mysteries by their very nature so excel the created intellect that, even when they have been communicated in revelation and received by faith, they remain covered by the veil of faith itself and shrouded as it were in darkness' (DC, p. 45).

On the other hand, however, there is an element in Roman Catholic theology that is resistant to any suggestion that doctrine attempts merely a vague approximation to the truth, since this would undermine its mission to teach authoritatively and (according to the logic of this tradition) inerrantly. The declaration *Mysterium Ecclesiae* warns against the view that 'dogmatic formulas (or some category of them) cannot signify truth in a determinate way, but can only offer changeable approximations to it which to a certain extent distort or alter it' and rejects the suggestion that these formulas 'signify the truth only in an indeterminate way' (DC, p. 61).

It is unfortunate, to say the least, that this statement should be so strikingly out of keeping with what modern philosophy of science tells us about the way in which our knowledge of the physical universe is acquired. It is an axiom of quantum physics that you cannot observe, or measure, subatomic particles without at the same time disturbing the object of your investigations and distorting the picture. The displacement effect of the human observer has to be taken into account at every step. This is perhaps a lesson that we would do well to extend from the sphere of quantum mechanics to the whole universe of knowledge - including theology where we have to reckon with the inescapable subjectivity of our knowledge of God.

Second, it is characteristic of modern scientific method to seek to persuade nature to disclose its secrets by means of ever more refined hypotheses, which, as they are perfected in the light of research, become progressively more adequate to the reality that they attempt to explain and, so to speak, gradually home in on it. In his recent writings, Karl Rahner has recognized that this tentative, hypothetical, revisable approach characterizes the whole of modern liberal culture and, for apologetic reasons, if for no other, the Church must adapt to respond to it. In Pannenberg's suggestive application of scientific method to the tasks of theology, Christian doctrines are regarded as hypotheses to elucidate the ultimate 'problem', the reality that determines all reality, the mystery of God.

Before going on to make the central affirmation of this chapter – that doctrines are adequate to the purpose that they are intended to fulfil – let us dwell for a moment on the character of doctrines and dogmas as, so to speak, incarnations of God's truth/reality in human nature.

Karl Rahner has gone much further than any official Roman Catholic statements in admitting the fragile, contingent and 'fallen' nature of the Church's teaching even within the sphere of revelation and the faith of the Church (V, p. 45). This, he recognizes, is a distinctively Reformation insight, tied up with Luther's formula concerning justification: *Simul iustus et peccator* (justified and sinful at the same time). Rahner makes it clear that there is a sense in which this formula is compatible with Catholic theology, provided due weight is also given to the truth that a Christian does not remain in perpetual bondage, a divided, tormented being, but is the subject of a new creation (VI, pp. 218-30).

Rahner goes yet further, suggesting that Luther's insight can be applied to the realm of the knowledge of God as well as to that of salvation. The fundamental paradox of justification, whereby God's saving purpose is carried out in and through and notwithstanding our mortal flesh, suggests the further paradox that the truth of God – his purpose to reveal himself to man – is carried out in and through and notwithstanding our sinful, circumscribed and stumbling intellects. Theological assertions may be adequate to their purpose as vehicles of the truth of God while remaining subject to all the limitations of the human mind.

If I understand him correctly, Rahner's carefully chosen words are intended to expose the futility and downright inappropriateness of the sort of either-right-or-wrong language employed by the Church's magisterium when pronouncing on questions of truth and error. 'One cannot brush aside the question as to whether dogmatic statements do not also bear the signature of guilty man in the state of original sin.' There is a theological coherence, a divine logic, in this position that, on the face of it, is essentially Evangelical and typical of Reformation theology. If, as Rahner himself clearly believes, it is also profoundly and authentically Catholic, we are given encouraging grounds for hope that a reconstruction of ecumenical theology is possible. The logic is to refer the ostensibly secondary and derivative principles of ecclesiology back to the primary and determinative principle of Christian theology, the incarnation. A view of the Church's teaching office and doctrinal formulas is seen to depend on a certain view of what is taking place in the realm of salvation, and that view of salvation is in turn seen to be dependent on a correct understanding of the incarnation, an acknowledgement of the true humanity of Christ. This constitutes the paradigm of what is to be believed regarding the truth-status of doctrines. As Rahner puts it, 'God's truth has also in reality incarnated itself into this flesh of sin' (V, p. 45).

What Michael Ramsey has called the 'perilous' character of the Church's teaching office and Rahner has described as the fallen nature of dogmatic statements, is reinforced when we consider the possibility, raised by Hans Küng, that pronouncements of the Church, delivered in a polemical context, may actually serve to perpetuate confusion between truth and error.

In line with Rahner's warning about the naivety of assuming that all propositions can be divided into those that are true and those that are false, Küng argues that 'every statement of truth borders on error due to its human limitations', with the result that every statement is open to both true and false interpretations (1965, pp. 350f; 1971a, pp. 140ff).

Küng's argument here has been criticized for giving philosophical hostages to fortune. The Lutheran theologian George Lindbeck, a member of the Lutheran-Roman Catholic conversations in the United States, for example, has asserted that Küng's position involves importing 'a highly speculative and technical philosophical view of truth' as the basis of his case against a false interpretation of infallibility. It may indeed be the case that Küng has been strongly influenced here by a Hegelian metaphysic that, in the present philosophical climate, would tend to bring discredit on his entire argument. But it is perfectly possible to understand Küng's point against a different background where it would command wider agreement.

It is an old adage, much favoured by irenical thinkers within the Anglican tradition such as Coleridge, Maurice and Temple, that people are usually right in what they affirm and often wrong in what they deny. In positive, affirmative statements we are expressing an authentic insight, born of personal experience, and therefore likely to contain a high proportion of truth. In negative, condemnatory, dismissive statements, on the other hand, we are reacting to views that we do not hold ourselves but attribute to others. The possibility of misunderstanding the other person's point of view is undoubtedly a real one.

This consideration is reinforced if we bear in mind the point made in an earlier chapter that expressions of belief belong not in the realm of theory, as speculative statements that in principle could be refuted by the evidence or by some crushing counter-argument, but in the realm of praxis where they express a personal conviction and commitment arising out of one's unique experience of what it is to be a human being in the world. Küng is certainly working on this assumption when he claims that, 'since every error, no matter how great, contains the kernel of some truth, a polemically orientated utterance is in danger of striking not only at the error, but also at the error's kernel of truth' (1965, p. 350).

The particular example that Küng offers - one that certainly carries conviction - is the Reformation and Counter-Reformation controversy over justification by faith. The point we are making here would seem to be borne out when we discover that the Council of Trent's anathemas against the Protestant doctrine of justification by faith were in fact directed at the notion of justification by a vain, boastful self-confidence that we are justified - a misunderstanding of the Reformers' teaching. There is all the more reason then to heed the admonition of the Church of England's Doctrine Commission that statements of doctrine should be (the words are A.E. Harvey's) 'provisional, tentative and infrequent' (1981, p. 290).

Adequacy Affirmed

Christian doctrines, as we have seen, are human imaginative constructs, elicited by moments of divine disclosure and shaped in conformity to established truth by being located within a tradition embodying a corporate and historical response to revelation. As the products of human reflection they can never be adequate to the transcendent reality to which they refer. But they do, nevertheless, correspond to that reality. Their inevitably human and mundane character does not render them false.

The constructive power of reason, whereby we are enabled to transcend sensation in perception and perception in judgement and judgement in creative speculation shot through with insight with its truth-seeking capability that 'homes in' on its target, is our mandate for affirming that Christian doctrines are adequate to their intended purpose. Their purpose is not to furnish us with an exhaustive and inerrant theoretical description of a reality external to ourselves, about which we may make a detached and impersonal assessment. It is to make us 'wise unto salvation . . . through faith' (2 Tim. 3.15). It is to effect a communication between a transcendently personal God and created personal beings, to convey a declaration of love and acceptance on the one hand, and to express an attitude of adoration and an intention of commitment, on the other. I would not go so far as Rahner does in claiming *a priori* that doctrines of the Church contain nothing that is actually false (1, pp. 43ff). As I have made clear earlier, I think there are degrees of inadequacy that are so misleading that they pass over into falsehood. And we need to be aware that Rahner has an elusive idealist or Platonic notion of the Church that entails that what it affirms in essence is not necessarily the same as its empirical utterances. But I would certainly want to endorse his

50

point that when we affirm the truth of Christian doctrine, we mean that it does indeed correspond to reality, although it is not simply congruent with it. Christian doctrine is true. But it is necessary to add this: it would be as misleading to say it was in any circumstances inerrant as to say that it was simply false.

The Church certainly requires an authority that is adequate to its task of teaching and guiding the faithful. My argument that this does not depend on a guarantee of inerrancy can be aptly illustrated by a comparison with the authority of scripture.

Anglicanism, as is to be expected of a church whose theology was shaped by Reformation principles, has always upheld the supreme authority of the Scriptures in the Church. The advance of biblical criticism, which has been virtually unfettered in Anglicanism for more than a century, has not significantly altered this in practice. But the Anglican confessional documents fortunately do not contain any claim that the Scriptures are infallible or inerrant, but content themselves with asserting that they 'contain all things necessary to salvation'. It is in line with this that Richard Hooker, in the *Ecclesiastical Polity*, refers the scope of scriptural authority to the divine intention to make known to us the way of salvation (I, xiv, 1f). Beyond this there is room for the Church to exercise its freedom 'to decree rites or ceremonies' and to employ its 'authority in controversies of faith', provided that its decisions are not incompatible with the tenor of biblical teaching or imposed on the conscience of Christians as being necessary to salvation.

The English Reformers teach that the Church exercises its intrinsic authority not only in rites, ceremonies and things indifferent, but also in controversies of faith, in disputed questions of doctrine. The Church has, however, no authority to put forward as necessary to salvation or as an article of faith anything except what is 'expressly contained in the word of God, or may manifestly thereof be gathered'. In other words, nothing is to be enforced as binding on the Church except what is contained in the word of God.

In establishing the supreme authority of Scripture and delimiting the scope of church authority in this way, the

Anglican Church acknowledges an adequacy, sufficiency and authority of Scripture that is not dependent on any supposed inerrancy, and an adequacy, sufficiency and authority of the Church in its proper sphere that is not dependent on any supposed infallibility.

The Roman Catholic position is not as clear cut. While recent statements do indeed assert the supreme authority of Scripture as the final standard of Christian doctrine, the tradition also contains emphatic assertions of the infallibility and inerrancy of Scripture – adding moreover, that this is not confined to matters of salvation or questions affecting faith and morals. The encyclical of Leo XIII, *Providentissimus Deus* (1893), for example, which did much to free Catholic biblical scholarship from outdated scholastic methods, nevertheless draws the line at admitting the presence of error in any form in the biblical documents, and rejects as intolerable the view that inerrant divine inspiration can be confined to the realm of faith and morals. The encyclical substantiates this position by reference to a dictation-theory of divine inspiration: 'For all the books in their entirety . . . have been written under the dictation of the Holy Spirit,' and 'it is utterly impossible that divine inspiration could contain any error' (DC, p. 78). The decree *Lamentabili* (1907) by which the movement of Catholic Modernism was suppressed, reiterated this position, asserting that every part of Scripture was preserved from error by divine inspiration.

More recent statements have seen a retreat from this position, in line with the limitations surrounding papal infallibility as defined by the First Vatican Council, where the infallibility of the Pope is attributed to divine assistance, not inspiration, and is restricted to 'doctrine concerning faith or morals'. The phrasing here obviously excludes from the protected realm of infallibility anything touching the sphere of natural knowledge which could be shown to be erroneous by the advance of science. But it is still significantly wider than the area of things 'necessary to salvation' of the Anglican formularies.

Vatican II moved perceptibly towards the more cautious

position reflected in the Thirty-Nine Articles. It gave up the notion of divine dictation and made allowance for the human element in the composition of the Scriptures. While still speaking in terms of inerrancy, it nevertheless referred this to God's purpose of salvation. According to the decree on revelation, 'Since everything asserted by the inspired authors or sacred writers must be held to be asserted by the Holy Spirit, it follows that the books of Scripture must be acknowledged as teaching firmly, faithfully, and without error that truth which God wanted put into the sacred writings for the sake of our salvation.' In an attempt to discourage the misuse of proof texts to settle questions of natural knowledge, the decree underlines the fact that the interpretation, as well as the inspiration of Scripture must be referred to the divine purpose of salvation. The interpreter of Scripture, 'in order to see clearly what God wanted to communicate to us, should carefully investigate what meaning the sacred writers really intended, and what God wanted to manifest by means of their words' (V2, pp. 119f).

It is significant, however, that *Mysterium Ecclesiae* reverted to speaking of 'faith and morals' rather than of truths necessary to salvation, when upholding the so called 'certain shared infallibility' of the whole Church, maintained in divine truth through the Holy Spirit. In this recent statement, as in the dominant assertions of the tradition, authority is regarded as ultimately dependent on infallibility, and infallibility is interpreted in terms of factual inerrancy. But, given the freer atmosphere in Roman Catholic biblical studies, presaged by the encyclical of Pius XII *Divine Afflante Spiritu* (1943), this position is bound to change.

What we must look for within Catholic theology now is a closer integration between the understanding of biblical authority in which God-given guarantees of truth (whether understood in terms of divine assistance, inspiration or actual inerrancy) have been reduced to matters directly affecting our salvation, and the understanding of the authority of the Church's teaching office, whose scope still embraces all matters of faith and morals (since in practice this includes all aspects of the beliefs and lives of Christians).

As far as ecumenical dialogue is concerned we may hope that all mention of inerrancy, however restricted, may be quietly abandoned on the Anglican side, even if this means that ecumenical reports like that of ARCIC may have to revert to setting out clearly the points of intractible difference instead of seeking to construct 'common statements' that sometimes serve to conceal the difficulties that still remain. One point is certain: the day is past when Newman could support the infallibility of the teaching Church by appealing to the - universally acknowledged - infallibility of Scripture (1974, p. 170). The adequacy of Scripture as the supreme authority for Christian doctrine is a paradigm of the nature of authority in all its forms in the Church.

Probability or Certainty?

Although no guarantee of inerrancy is given to her, when the Church reaches a common mind (and we shall shortly see how this precondition restricts the possibilities), its teaching merits a presumption of truth. The weight of probability is that she is on the right track. For traditionalist Roman Catholics this will seem a provokingly minimalist statement, but for Anglicans it is as much as they have a right to ask. The Anglican tradition accepts that probability is the highest degree of certainty that we may hope to enjoy in this world. It regards the rule of faith (*regula fidei*) as a set of practical guidelines.

The doctrine of probability goes back to the roots of Anglicanism in the writings of Richard Hooker, who points out in the *Ecclesiastical Polity* that, though the human mind craves 'the most infallible certainty which the nature of things can yield', assent must always be proportionate to the evidence. Hooker observes that there are various gradations of certainty, from intuition at the highest ('intuitive beholding') where the truth is its own evidence and we can entertain no other view of the matter, through demonstration or proof where the conclusion is entailed in the premisses, to mere probability where we become convinced by the weight of the evidence. Hooker concludes that in the absence of infallible proof, which the nature of things does not usually afford, the mind must allow itself to be guided by 'probable persuasions' (II, vii, 5).

In his great treatise *Of the Church*, Richard Field, Hooker's contemporary and fellow architect of Anglican ecclesiology, renounces the futile quest for guarantees of truth in the Church and develops a concept of probability. For Field, general councils are no more and no less directed by the Holy Spirit than other major synods of the Church and 'are not led to the finding out of the truth in any special sort or manner beyond the general influence that is required to the performance of every good work.' While, therefore, there is no guarantee that the majority view of the bishops gathered together in a general council will be the true one, where a council is comprehensively and regularly constituted, its decisions merit a presumption of truth (V, c, 1ii).

From the Cambridge Platonists and Jeremy Taylor onwards, the notion of probability constantly surfaces during the seventeenth century. It receives its classical theological expression in Bishop Joseph Butler's celebrated *Analogy of Religion, Natural and Revealed* (1736). Butler is working within a common tradition that includes Hooker and finds a notable exponent in Locke. In the *Essay Concerning Human Understanding* (1690) Locke echoes Hooker's realistic sense of 'the nature of things', his doctrine of the degrees of certainty and his requirement to proportion assent to the strength of the evidence. If, Locke remarks in his introduction, we can ascertain the true extent and limitations of our knowledge, 'we may learn to content ourselves with what is attainable by us in this state'. There is also the sense that the restricted vision that we have is adequate to the essential questions of life: 'The candle that is set up in us shines bright enough for all our purposes' (I, p. 7). Though in many things probability is the most we can hope for, this degree of certainty 'is as great as our happiness or misery, beyond which we have no concernment to know or to be' (II, p. 144). Our human condition is a state of moral probation, in which certitude is largely denied us, and we are called to make our pilgrimage in the search for truth, with 'only the twilight . . . of probability' to light our way (II, pp. 247f).

In Bishop Butler's classical phrase, 'probability is the very guide of life', and the degree of certainty it affords is consonant with 'the very condition of our being' in this earthly state of moral probation (pp. 73, 315). Butler's doctrine of probability is not, as might appear, an attempt to settle upon the lowest common denominator (in his case, in the argument with eighteenth-century deism), but rather to clarify the highest degree of assurance consistent with the limitations of human knowledge, to which infallibility certainly is denied.

As Henry Scott Holland pointed out in his Romanes Lecture *The Optimism of Butler's 'Analogy'* (1908), the appeal to probability is not a negative, defeatist approach, but a highly positive, constructive one. For Butler, probability is equivalent to moral certainty. It is an attempt to combine rational and moral perceptions. It is precisely on moral grounds that a later Anglican thinker in the Butlerian tradition, A.E. Taylor, claims in his Gifford Lectures, *The Faith of a Moralist*, that true authority finds any claim to infallibility alien to its nature (II, pp. 228ff).

The faith of believers in God is like the faith of scientists in the reality they set out to explore. Their existential decision is like the scientists' commitment to the truth they seek. The doctrines that believers accept are like the hypotheses that scientists employ in their research. Scientists are certain of reality, they trust their hypotheses, but they do not confuse the two. In the same way it is vital to distinguish between the epistemological status of faith as an existential act, on the one hand, and the doctrines of 'the faith', on the other.

Faith knows nothing of probabilities but launches itself into the (explicitly) unknown in response to the (tacitly sensed) approach of its object, the divine reality. It is not faith itself, but reflection on faith formulated in doctrines, that is characterized by probability. Where faith is seen as merely assent to revealed truths, this fundamental distinction is obscured. We can illustrate this by reference to official Roman Catholic reaction to the Modernists and Newman's lifelong wrestling with this problem.

There is a significant affinity between the instincts of

Anglicanism and the position worked out by the Roman Catholic Modernists. Alfred Loisy, for example, wrote in *L'Évangile et l'Église* (1902), as cited by Reardon, 'The church does not exact belief in its formulas as the adequate expression of absolute truth, but presents them as the least imperfect expression that is morally possible' (p. 88). Accordingly, Loisy claimed, the decree *Lamentabili*, in suppressing Modernism, included in its syllabus of errors the view that 'the assent of faith ultimately rests on a mass of probabilities' (p. 245). Here however, the decree makes the mistake common to its genre of interpreting the views it condemns in terms of its own assumptions, not of theirs. For the Modernists, faith was not assent to propositional truths but a practical, personal commitment. As a response of the whole person, it was not a calculated step proportioned to the evidence and resting on an assessment of probabilities, but an existential act based on moral certainty – a certainty that is an attribute of the believer, not of the statements in which the beliefs held might be expressed. Probability resides not in faith (which speaks the language of certitude) but in the adequacy of doctrinal statements as descriptions of a transcendent reality.

A similar ambiguity can be detected in Newman's wrestlings with this question. Newman takes Locke and Butler as his point of departure and examines the question of probability and certainty in the terms that they had laid down. But he eventually parts company with Locke by claiming that probable arguments can yield subjective certainty about truths of doctrine. This marked his break not only with Locke but with Hooker and Butler – in fact with the Anglican theological method.

In *The Prophetical Office of the Church* (1837) Newman is still the disciple of Butler, and the architect of Tractarian theology. 'We for our part,' he declares, 'have been taught to consider that in its degree faith, as well as conduct, must be guided by probabilities, and that doubt is ever our portion in this life' (p. 108). In the 1845 essay on development, however, Newman makes a significant move. He argues for an infallible defining authority in the Church and withdraws his earlier objection to infallibility (one that goes back to Chillingworth) that the principle can itself claim no more than probability (pp. 76, 168ff). In the *Grammar of Assent* Newman clarifies his position, making faith an existential act. Because he is still working with the notion of divinely revealed truths in propositional form, he has to expand the idea of assent to accommodate his enlarged understanding of faith, but it cannot take the strain.

Religion makes a total demand upon our commitment and calls us to suffer for its sake. A mere 'balance of arguments' can never produce absolute self-dedication. Personal sacrifice, mastery of self and 'communion with the spiritual world', Newman asserts, presuppose a strength of spiritual conviction that amounts to 'certitude under another name' (p. 238). Even in human matters, life can only go on because we are able to take so many things for granted. Strictly speaking they may be probabilities, but they are 'probabilities founded on certainties'. In matters human and divine, Newman concludes, we have 'indefectible certitude in primary truths' and 'manifold variations of opinion in their application and disposition' (pp. 239f).

Newman's position suggests two observations. First, he has quite clearly transferred certainty from propositions to the mind that holds them (Naulty, p. 456). This is quite conclusively where it belongs. Thus we may feel subjectively certain about something that is objectively only probable. But this consideration, it seems to me, undermines any grounds for speaking of infallibility as an attribute of teachings, propositions or even persons acting in a particular capacity. It is interesting to note that Peter Chirico has taken this logic a step further in his treatise on infallibility where he appears to regard infallibility as a state of mind. We may *feel* infallibly certain, that is all. Infallibility belongs therefore to the area of the psychology of religion, not to the doctrines of revelation or authority.

Secondly, working with the Platonic distinction between knowledge and mere opinion, Newman restricts 'indefectible certainty' to 'primary truths' that are not subject to 'manifold variations of opinion' but command immediate and general assent. But is anyone prepared to claim today that the notion of the infallibility of the Church or the Pope belongs to the primary truths of Christianity? Is it not abundantly clear that this is a contested doctrine that belongs in the category of opinion where there will be a wide variety of views? If this is so, the doctrine of infallibility and its concomitants ought to be deleted from the agenda of doctrines essential as a platform for unity between the Anglican and Roman Catholic Churches, and some form or degree of unity ought to be pursued that does not depend on agreement on this point.

To return in conclusion to the Anglican approach: Anglicanism enshrines a principle of reverent agnosticism. It takes seriously the limitations of our knowledge and readily confesses that our grasp of the truth is circumscribed by mystery, a light shining in the darkness. We cannot know whether the Church, at any given time, is in possession of the truth, or whether what the Pope decides in a particular case is free from error, or even whether the emergence in history of the papacy is attributable to divine providence.

Anglicanism appeals, in the words of the second-generation Tractarian R.W. Church, to 'reality, history and experience' (1891, p. 346). It finds unpalatable the sort of unverifiable assumptions, grandiose claims and triumphalist mentality that, although in a muted form, persist in the ARCIC *Final Report*. However, the Anglican appeal to reality, experience and 'how things are' is not a recipe for scepticism or a basis for a minimalist approach to doctrine, but exhibits a distinctive view of the dispensation in which we are called to make our pilgrimage, walking 'by faith not by sight'.

4

Consensus and Criticism

Contemporary understanding of the Church has acquired a new dimension. It has discovered the notion of 'the mind of the Church'. *Consensus fidelium* has now established itself as one of the key concepts of contemporary ecclesiology. After Vatican I, Roman Catholics - most notably Newman in *On Consulting the Faithful in Matters of Doctrine* - put forward the idea of the *consensus fidelium*, consent of the faithful, as a necessary corrective to the Council's one-sided stress on the defining authority of the Pope. Vatican II, in attempting to complete the doctrine of the magisterium that was abruptly broken off in Vatican I, gave priority to the notions of collegiality and consultation (though without, needless to say, retracting anything claimed by the First Council). Among Roman Catholic theologians, Karl Rahner has been notable in giving the cluster of ideas represented by the expression *consensus fidelium* his sustained attention in many writings.

Anglicans, for their part, made uncomfortably aware of the plurality of doctrinal positions within their own communion, have been asking - in Stephen Sykes' *The Integrity of Anglicanism* and the Doctrine Commission's report *Believing in the Church*, for example - whether there is a fundamental consensus among Anglicans as to what they stand for doctrinally.

In dialogue between Anglicans and Roman Catholics, Anglicans have seized upon the elements within contemporary Catholic ecclesiology that stress the need for attention to the consensus of faith and for reception of definitions by the faithful as offering a way round the intractable problem of papal authority and infallibility; while Catholics have energetically pushed these ideas to the fore, sensing that they represent for their partners in dialogue the acceptable face of Catholicism. As a result, 'the mind of the Church' has become one of the most overworked concepts of modern ecclesiology. It has been made to carry a weight that it was not intended (by Newman, for example) to bear.

The Mind of the Church

The ARCIC *Final Report* contemplates the Church making 'a decisive judgement in matters of faith' - a judgement which will 'exclude error' - in situations where 'serious divisions of opinion on crucial issues of pastoral urgency call for a more definitive judgement' than the routine and *ad hoc* pastoral communications of the ordinary magisterium (p. 93:27).

We might pause here to express astonishment at the accumulation of qualifications that the commission has built into this procedure. The divisions within the Church must be 'serious', the issues they reflect must be 'crucial', the pastoral implications must be 'urgent'. The procedure envisaged is evidently one of last resort and one that everyone hopes will never have to be used - like impeaching a President of the United States or unleashing one's nuclear missiles against an enemy.

Who seriously supposes that an issue of this magnitude that has split the Church is going to be resolved by a decision of the magisterium even after the fullest consultation? Who imagines that the side that has the decision go against it is going to lie down and accept that the matter is closed? Who in reality doubts that the magisterium itself - primarily the college of bishops of the world-wide Church - would also be fundamentally divided on the issue in question and unable to come to a common mind? Questions such as these make one wonder whether we are talking about the Church that actually exists on earth or merely about a Church that exists only on the drawing board - a conceptual construct designed to incorporate contradictory theories, to reconcile the irreconcilable.

Such a definitive judgement, the report continues, must be understood not only in the context of its time and place but also in the light of the Church's whole experience and tradition. To a certain extent, the mind of the Church is inevitably relative to the contemporary situation: 'All such definitions are provoked by specific historical situations and are always made in terms of the understanding and framework of their age.' But at the same time, the mind of the Church transcends the limitations of time and place in that its deliverances 'retain a lasting significance if they are safeguarding the substance of the faith' (p. 93:27). Here we have the difficult idea of a consensus of the moment subsisting in a broader and more permanent consensus that spans the life of the Church. Elusive though this concept appears to be at first sight, it may well be that it embodies a significant insight about the nature of tradition. But it certainly needs a great deal more analysis and refinement than the bald juxtapositions of the report provide.

The central difficulty for the Roman Catholic Church is that it is accustomed to appeal to a permanent consensus on such issues as contraception or the ordination of women where the current consensus seems to point in a different direction. If the current consensus is only valid when it agrees with the permanent consensus, there is no need for us to concern ourselves with it; it becomes wholly superfluous. This is the obvious logic of the failure of the authorities in Rome to implement the apparatus of consultation envisaged by the Second Vatican Council and of the extreme caution expressed in official Catholic theology about the notion of reception.

According to the ARCIC statement, whether the defining authority in this case is a general council or the universal primate, the whole Church is involved as it reflects upon and 'receives' the teaching that is dispensed for its consideration, coming eventually, as is hoped, to a common mind. The faithful will welcome the teaching as something they have known all along deep in their hearts. It will have the ring of truth. It will commend itself as 'what oft was thought but ne'er so well expressed'. Thus the report stresses that 'the church in all its members is involved in such a definition' which has the effect of 'clarifying and enriching their grasp of the truth' (p. 92:25). This last point needs to be looked at carefully.

In his treatise on infallibility, Peter Chirico has stressed the tacit nature of the Church's sense of faith (*sensus fidei*). Following Möhler and Newman who spoke of it as an 'instinct', he refers the *sensus fidei* to those 'universal Christian meanings that are implicitly embedded in the living faith' of Christians (p. 209). The magisterium on the other hand enjoys a special and rare charism which enables it to grasp explicitly and articulate these universal meanings that exist only tacitly in the spiritual sense of the faithful (*sensus fidelium*). The pronouncements of the hierarchy are intended to render this explicit. This is their *raison d'être*. and the purpose of this exercise is, as Chirico remarks, 'to strengthen and deepen the sense of faith in all; for a meaning becomes more operative in one's life for having been made explicit' (pp. 209, 214).

I want to return at a later stage of this chapter to the question of the tacit nature of the consensus of faith. For the present I will merely raise two questions about the assumptions behind the view of ARCIC and Chirico that the magisterium makes explicit what is implicit in the *sensus fidelium*.

First, if the consensus exists only tacitly it is obviously no simple matter to consult it, to sound it out on disputed issues, as ARCIC envisages. But perhaps that is not what it is there for. Perhaps, as Newman believed, the content of the sense of faith, 'deep in the bosom of the mystical body of Christ', is concerned with the great credal affirmations of Christianity, not with their application to pastoral problems, however serious. For Newman it provided protection from doctrinal error, through the working of the Holy Spirit, the Spirit of truth. It operated in the realm of principles: 'Submit your heretical and Catholic principle[s] to the action of the multitude and you will be able to pronounce at once whether it is imbued with Catholic truth or with heretical falsehood' (1961, pp. 73ff). The notion of correlating the tacit *sensus fidelium* with the explicit formulations of the magisterium, as proposed by Chirico and ARCIC, remains problematic.

Second, is the tacit always capable of being rendered explicit, and if so, is this invariably a good thing? Does it make sense to attempt to translate poetry into prose, myth into the historical or unhistorical, expressions of love into descriptions of psychological states, liturgy into doctrine? Common sense answers No, and the teaching of Michael Polanyi on the tacit dimension of knowledge as the source of creativity and discovery confirms that answer.

These considerations lead us to question the validity of ARCIC's claim that a formal definition by the magisterium, articulating the mind of the Church, will have the effect of 'clarifying and enriching' our 'grasp of the truth' (p. 92:25). This assertion contains several dubious assumptions.

First of all, it is not self-evident that the truth is susceptible of being clarified. It is a rationalist fallacy that truth and clarity go hand in hand and that the clearer we become in our own minds, the closer to the truth we are. This give-away phrase 'clarifying and enriching' confirms my impression that the report is working with an inadequate idea of the nature of truth.

Second, it follows that the report's juxtaposition of 'clarify' and 'enrich' should be viewed with scepticism. There appears to be an implied contradiction here. We do not normally think of these two terms as complementary, indeed often the reverse. Sometimes a matter needs clarifying; sometimes it needs enriching, but not both at once. Consider these words in the light of history. Can we think of authoritative pronouncements of the magisterium that have purported to 'clarify' issues but in reality have put a stop to all discussion?: from Vatican I, *Pastor Aeternus* on papal infallibility; the Marian dogmas; the suppression of Catholic modernism and biblical criticism; the condemnation of artificial methods of birth control. 'Clarify' is often an authoritarian euphemism for 'restrict'.

Third, I cannot accept that to make explicit the unarticulated, unanalysed faith of lay Christians – a faith that is more felt than thought – is necessarily going to result in the enrichment of that faith. I am not disparaging hard thinking, rigorous analysis, systematic construction. This is the calling of the theologian – to get things as clear as they can be, to obtain a grasp of the internal coherence of the Christian faith, to follow through the implications of what all Christians profess in worship and life. But there is a price to be paid for this, and some theologians have made a real sacrifice of personal assurance in following the truth wherever it leads. Just as individual theologians are sustained in their intellectual task by the deep springs of faith within (which are not necessarily enhanced by the labour of explication), so the theological task of the Church itself is dependent on - even parasitic on - the implicit faith of the whole Christian body. It is not called to bring it into its own image. The faith of Christians is a delicate flower. If we try to clarify it too much we run the risk of clarifying it right away. If this faith needs enrichment, it is not going to receive it from the official statements of the Church's teaching authority - formal, binding, infallible, beyond question: what could be less conducive to spiritual enrichment than that? - but rather from mutual fellowship in joy or sorrow, from the resources of the liturgy, from music and literature. These are the stimuli that deepen, enhance and enrich the faith of Christians. Newman understood these matters when he consistently claimed that superstition was preferable to sophistication where faith was concerned.

Regarding the role of the magisterium, there is one more statement of the report that requires comment. The involvement of all church members in the promulgation of an authoritative definition is, according to ARCIC, reciprocal. While, on the one hand, their own faith will benefit in clarity and enrichment from the teaching of the magisterium, 'their active reflection upon the definition in its turn clarifies its significance' (p. 92:25). It is wonderful how opaque statements about clarity can be! This must be one of the most elusive propositions in the work of the commission. It makes one wonder how to take the disclaimers of studied ambiguity that its members put out from time to time. If statements like this are not intentionally slippery, they must be unintentionally so - leading us to ask, Was this the best that they could do?

The statement appears in the report without any expansion or elucidation so we have to do our best to unwrap it. Two phrases call for comment: 'active reflection' and 'clarifies its significance'. 'Active reflection' sounds like a bland periphrasis for 'criticism' in its proper sense of interpretation and evalua-

65

tion - as in literary criticism or musical criticism. The report does not grapple with criticism in the popular sense of pointing out what is wrong. That has to be left to Catholic theologians like Rahner and Küng who have laid the duty of criticism upon the Church in no uncertain terms. That critical evaluation is not the intention of the report, however, is clear from what immediately follows: 'it is not through reception by the people of God that a definition first acquires authority'. A definition comes bearing the stamp of authority; we must take it or leave it; we cannot ask for its credentials; what we are called to do is to accept it in a spirit of intelligent and informed appreciation. This is how its 'significance' is 'clarified'. When the faithful receive it, as they surely will, it is revealed to be an authentic definition of the Church's God-given teaching authority.

This is as far as we can go in attempting to interpret this delphic utterance of the report, and it leads immediately to the question of reception by the faithful as presented by ARCIC and as taught in recent Catholic theology.

Reception by the Faithful

Having said that reception by the faithful does not endow a definition with authority, for it must possess this in itself by virtue of its truth, the ARCIC report goes on to enunciate the principle of *reception*. 'The assent of the faithful is the ultimate indication that the Church's authoritative decision in a matter of faith has been truly preserved from error by the Holy Spirit. The Holy Spirit who maintains the Church in the truth will bring its members to receive the definition as true and to assimilate it if what has been declared genuinely expounds the revelation' (p. 92:25).

Obviously, the confidence of the report in this matter presupposes a certain view of the indefectibility of the Church and of the nature of truth. The document follows the line adopted by the Second Vatican Council which, while wary of the doctrine of reception, did stress the infallible instinct of the faithful, inspired by the Holy Spirit, which leads them to embrace the truths enunciated by the magisterium. The Constitution on the Church declares: 'The body of the faithful as a whole, anointed as they are by the Holy One . . . cannot err in matters of belief'. Citing Augustine, the Constitution goes on to claim that, 'thanks to a supernatural sense of the faith which characterizes the People as a whole, it manifests this unerring quality when, "from the bishops down to the last member of the laity", it shows universal agreement in matters of faith and morals' (V2, p. 29). When the magisterium – the bishops together with the Pope – formally utters its mind, the assent of the Church will surely be forthcoming through the work of the Holy Spirit, 'whereby the whole flock of Christ is preserved and progresses in unity of faith' (V2, p. 49).

The Declaration *Mysterium Ecclesiae* issued in 1973 by the Sacred Congregation for the Doctrine of the Faith with the backing of Pope Paul VI in order to combat subversive theologians, especially Hans Küng, speaks in the same vein of 'the unhesitating assent of the People of God concerning matters of faith and morals'. Although our obedience is ultimately to God himself, our 'conversion to God through faith' is itself 'a form of obedience' and shows itself in submission to the revelation that is mediated to us through the infallible teaching of the Church's pastors. Our conversion to God therefore takes the form of adhering to him 'in the integral doctrine of the Catholic faith' (DC, pp. 248f).

Karl Rahner has produced a critique of *Mysterium Ecclesiae* which will serve as a convenient stepping-stone to his thought on the question of consensus and reception. He raises several pertinent questions concerning the further statement of the declaration that there is 'a certain shared infallibility', restricted to matters of faith and morals, 'which is present when the whole people of God unhesitatingly holds a point of doctrine pertaining to these matters.'

The question Rahner raises about the notion of 'shared' infallibility and what precisely is meant by this – what delimitation of roles between magisterium and the faithful does it imply? – is one for purely internal consumption within the Roman Catholic Church. But Rahner also asks whether the criterion of a conviction being 'unhesitatingly held' is adequate, considering that many convictions unhesitatingly held throughout the Church from time to time have later been abandoned and would now be regarded as mistaken. He goes on to question whether the notion of 'the whole people of God' is an 'empirically comprehensible entity'. Only if it can be claimed convincingly that it is empirically cashable does it have relevance for determining the character of Christian faith (XVII, p. 143).

Rahner's view of consensus and the process of reception has not always been so cautious. In the early 1960s he was expressing somewhat sanguine views about the possibilities of a consensus of faith. Writing after the promulgation of the dogma of the Assumption of Mary but before *Humanae Vitae* with its condemnation of modern methods of birth control, Rahner felt able to claim that a papal definition had never been given where the object of the definition was not already believed by the Church as a truth of faith. He envisages in an idealistic way the process whereby the Church comes to know its own mind: 'The church as a whole considers a thought which grows out of the whole content of its faith: it ripens, it merges ever more fully with the whole, while the church lives it and perfects it. And so the church of a certain day, if we may say so, finds itself simply there, believing in this special manner' (IV, pp. 31f). The Church will therefore receive the definitions of authority because it already tacitly believes them. The paper definition that follows simply ratifies what is already a fact. A truth 'has impressed itself slowly and without flourish of trumpets on the believing consciousness of the church.'

Rahner's persuasive version of the role of the Pope in this process would, so it appears, receive the endorsement of the Anglican-Roman Catholic Commission. For Rahner, 'the Pope is the point at which the collective consciousness of the whole church attains effective self-awareness' as a focus of authority for its individual members. In his latest published writings Rahner reiterates this view, describing the Pope as 'the authentic spokesman of the church's sense of faith', whose infallibility stems from 'his appeal to the infallible sense of faith of the church as a whole' (XX, pp. 137f). Along the same lines, the *Final Report* reached agreement on the role of the Pope as the one who can articulate the mind of the Church after full consultation, and do so in a way that is divinely preserved from error. Significantly, precisely the same idea is presented in Jean Tillard's recent book *The Bishop of Rome* (Tillard is, of course, a member of the Commission), where the 'infallible judgement' of the Pope 'articulates and brings to full expression the "instinctively right" . . . judgements of the people of God.' However, Tillard's comment that this is an example of 'the phenomenon of corporate personality . . . at work' may be taken with a pinch of salt! (p. 177).

The thrust of Rahner's argument is obviously slightly different from that of the report. He is seeking to curb the propensity of the magisterium to multiply authoritative definitions, by limiting its role to that of articulating what has already emerged in the collective mind of the Church. The report, on the other hand, is attempting to find a place for papal authority in a united church in a form that safeguards the appeal to reason and the duty of private judgement that are vital to the Anglican tradition. There is, therefore, a difference of emphasis that ought not to be overlooked between progressive Catholic ecclesiologists such as Rahner, who call for a wide-ranging process of consultation within the Church *before* any definition is uttered, on the one hand, and Anglican ecumenical proposals that bend over backwards in the attempt to reach agreement by postulating a process of evaluation in the Church at large *subsequent* to the definition, on the other.

It is also significant that, while the report is happy to rest a great deal on the concept of consensus, Rahner himself has moved – as the later volumes of the *Theological Investigations* testify – to a much less sanguine view of the possibility of widespread agreement in the Church. This is due largely to his growing sombre awareness of the intractable problems of pluralism, and partly to the shock administered to progressive Catholic theology in its post-Vatican II euphoria by the papal encyclical *Humanae Vitae* of 1968, which conspicuously did *not* reflect the mind of the Church.

ARCIC's emphasis on reception by the faithful to validate (in the elusive sense of this concept employed in the *Final Report*) the decisions of the magisterium is also vulnerable from another angle. It involves a circular argument. The report is confident that the Holy Spirit 'who maintains the church in the truth' will guide the faithful to accept such a decision if it 'genuinely expounds the revelation' (p. 92:25). This reflects closely the view presented by Peter Chirico:

> The only way the church can be sure that a pope or council has spoken infallibly is by finding the meaning proclaimed actually present in the consciousness of the faithful. Only when the vast numbers of the faithful discover that the meaning of a proclamation resonates with the meaning of the faith within them . . . can the church be assured that its authorities have spoken infallibly (p. 241).

In other words, whatever can be said to be both taught by the magisterium and accepted by the faithful is *ipso facto* revealed as being divine truth. Or, to put it another way, we can know that the magisterium has been preserved from error by the Holy Spirit (as ARCIC puts it) when we see that its decisions are received by the faithful, because we are here presupposing that the faithful themselves will be preserved from error by the same Spirit.

One reply to this would be to point to historical examples of both magisterium and faithful agreeing on some fundamental tenet that one side later repudiated. Hans Küng has done this in the case of birth control in his celebrated diatribe *Infallible?* Who can deny, he asks, that such a consensus has existed for centuries, that artificial methods of birth control have been consistently condemned in recent times by numerous episcopal conferences and individual bishops giving judgement? Küng points out that the conservative minority on the papal commission – the commission whose recommendations were, notoriously, rejected by Pope Paul VI in *Humanae Vitae* - was able to point out that 'history provides the fullest evidence . . . that the answer of the church has always and everywhere been the same, from the beginning up to the present decade'. 'One can find', it continues, 'no period of history, no document of the church, no theological school, scarcely one Catholic theologian, who ever denied that contraception was always seriously evil.' The conservatives were able therefore to conclude that the Church's teaching on contraception was 'absolutely constant' (p. 54). The universal consent – classically expressed in the canon of St Vincent of Lerins, *semper, ubique et ab omnibus*, 'always, everywhere and by all' – on the question of birth control has broken down in our lifetime, not because the magisterium changed its mind, but because the faithful – who after all were the ones who had to put it into practice – found the traditional view impossible.

This process is now being repeated in the matter of the ordination of women to the priesthood. In October 1976 the Sacred Congregation for the Doctrine of the Faith published with the approval of Pope Paul VI a 'Declaration on the Question of the Admission of Women to the Ministerial Priesthood'. It would be superfluous to say on which side of the argument the declaration came down! But it began by referring to the 'unbroken tradition throughout the history of the church, universal in the East and in the West', which indisputably and invariably excluded women from the priest-hood. This was an unquestioned axiom of the Church which had never before required the intervention of the magisterium to defend it. (The Sacred Congregation for the Doctrine of the Faith's *Observations* on the *Final Report* invoke the constant tradition alleged by this *Declaration* of 1976 as a barrier to union with a communion that ordains women.)

In criticizing the declaration, Karl Rahner makes the point that tradition is not a *carte blanche* that can be invoked to give an imprimatur to anything that has been taken for granted and remained unquestioned for centuries. Not all tradition is necessarily a vehicle of divine revelation which would be absolutely and definitively binding on the Church. There is obviously, he says, 'a purely human' tradition in the Church which offers no guarantee of truth even if it has long gone unchallenged (XX, pp. 35ff).

The criterion of consensus is not by itself a sufficient

guarantee of divine truth. To appeal to a consensus which is by definition historically and empirically verifiable is to give hostages to fortune. But since awkward historical facts seem to have a minimal deterrent effect on the manufacture of dogma, a more conclusive reply to the ARCIC report's assertions about the *consensus fidei* would be simply to point out that it is (not viciously, but perhaps trivially) circular and therefore inconclusive.

Once we give up the view that consensus in the Church is - under certain ascertainable circumstances - a firm guarantee of the truth, we can go on to recognize the fact that consensus as such is a purely *neutral* concept. It is not a good in itself. It is capable of being informed with truth or blinded by error and ignorance.

Translated into political terms, consensus is mandatory in a democracy under the rule of law. This is the grain of truth in the idea of 'consensus politics': in a democracy, government rules by consent. But it does not follow that the right political prescription for a nation's ills is to be found in the 'middle ground', any more than theological truth is to be found by seeking a *via media*. It is simply an acknowledgement of the fact that you have to carry the people with you. On the other hand, there is no need to assume that a consensus is inherently suspect - as though the minority is always right. This is an assumption, moreover, that is as often as not tinged with disdain *de haut en bas* (whether based on class or intellectual superiority) for the ignorant masses in their Gadarene descent into prejudice and superstition.

A consensus, like any other ideological construct, is not purely the product of the object to which it ostensibly refers, but is conditioned by all sorts of extraneous influences - social, cultural, political and economic. Thus a consensus in the Church concerning some question of doctrine or ethics will incorporate not only the response of the faithful to God's revelation of his love in Jesus Christ, but also distortions of this revelation as it is communicated to us through the human and impersonal channels of history, as well as constraints upon our response by factors which are more appropriately studied by the social sciences than by theology. This is why, as Charles Davis and Nicholas Lash have argued, ideological criticism must be taken to the heart of the Christian theological enterprise, so that both the prevailing consensus among the faithful and the specific teachings of the magisterium may become subject to its discipline and so purged of any unworthy elements that serve to pervert the truth of God.

It is salutary to remind ourselves that consensus is not a good in itself but morally neutral, becoming a good only when it is consensus in the truth. It is then transformed from mere consensus into the theological concept of *catholicity*. Whether a consensus in the Church on any given issue is equivalent to catholicity can only be known with any degree of assurance by appeal to objective sources of verification: historical, exegetical, ethical, philosophical.

Both Orthodox and Reformation theology can be cited in support of this view. Orthodox theology regards the Church's instinct for the truth (*sensus ecclesiae*) as the seat of a practical infallibility that preserves the whole people of God in the truth. This *sensus ecclesiae* must be allowed to exercise a monitoring function on any consensus that may emerge in the Church. John Meyendorff has shown how this works in the case of Augustinianism - which Orthodoxy rejects. In the western tradition, he writes, Augustine 'has been isolated from the entire tradition of the church and considered as the unique source of theological knowledge.' Thus, Meyendorff asserts, 'a new synthesis and a new consensus took place' that was not compatible with the received Greek patristic theology. The Orthodox reject this synthesis, he concludes, not because of its novelty - since, as Meyendorff significantly admits, 'new theologies, new formulations of doctrine' are unavoidable - but because it is found wanting when brought to the bar of independent assessment in the light of the gospel as we find it in Scripture and the Fathers (pp. 137, 148). Thus, in the Orthodox understanding, as Meyendorff presents it, mere consensus is no guarantee of truth, but needs to be evaluated by the theological criteria based on Scripture and patristic theology.

For the Reformers and the Anglican divines who followed them, catholicity is defined in relation to truth, not in relation to consent as such (nor, as they polemically asserted, to the universal jurisdiction of the papacy). Inward possession of truth was prized above outward imposition of unity. The Reformers warned against the real possibility of consensus in error. As John Jewel pointed out, 'There was the greatest consent that might be amongst them that worshipped the golden calf and among them who with one voice jointly cried against our Saviour Jesus Christ, "Crucify him!"' And as Sandys quaintly remarked, 'Adam and Eve and the serpent were all of one mind'! For all the Reformers – and here the English divines quoted are merely representative – consensus is only equivalent to catholicity when it is founded on truth. As Bradford put it, 'Unity must be in verity.'

The ARCIC report seems to envisage a teaching authority with sufficient flexibility to respond immediately to any pressing issues that may arise within the Church. It will gird up its loins to tackle the matter without delay. Its considered judgement (the report takes for granted that it will be able to reach one), will then be submitted to a streamlined process of consultation and reception by the Church at large.

This scenario bears little relation to reality. It is highly implausible that the magisterium would have the ability to come to grips with the sort of urgent pastoral problems that the report seems to have in mind. It is unlikely that its eventual response would have the decisiveness required to settle the issue. However, supposing for a moment that the hierarchy did manage to achieve a swift and decisive response, the momentum would immediately be lost in the inevitably slow and cumbersome process of reception by the faithful. There is no way in which a common mind can emerge in the Church with the rapidity that is needed to deal with pressing issues.

In his 'Dream of the Church', Karl Rahner has described the range of consultation that would be required if a judgement of the magisterium were to qualify as a true reflection of the mind of the Church. Such a process of consultation could not take place behind closed doors, 'in smoke-filled rooms', where concessions were extracted and bargaining counters traded. Of course Rahner does not say this in so many words; he is much more diplomatic. What he calls for is explicit, transparent, straightforward, sincere and public dialogue. There would have to be discussions with theologians, consultation of the world-wide episcopate, and conversations with the leaders of churches that had entered into union schemes with Rome while retaining their essential independence. Rahner optimistically concludes: 'With such procedures even non-Catholic Christians would no longer need to fear an arbitrary manipulation of the papal teaching authority opposed to the Spirit of Jesus and of the Church' (XX, p. 138).

That may be so, but the question that needs to be asked is, would the result be worth having? Would not the area of eventual agreement be so restricted as to amount to a statement of the obvious?

This leads us to observe that the statements of the magisterium, dependent as they are on the consensus of the whole Church, will be necessarily conservative. In other words, they will be platitudes. This is not to say that the Church has no teaching office – it must offer the gospel to the world and enunciate the primary truths of Christianity. Nor is it to disparage the notion of the mind of the Church – provided we do not attempt to put it to uses for which it is not adapted. Neither is it to dismiss the Church, on account of its conservative character, as irrelevant to the needs and questions of the modern world. Religion, bound up as it is with tradition and a community, is essentially conservative in nature; it is concerned with abiding truths and realities that will never pass away; and that is precisely where its relevance to a bewildered and fretful world lies. But the argument certainly does effectively undermine the hope expressed by the ARCIC report that the teaching office of the Church will be enabled 'to show how Christian truth applies to contemporary issues' (p. 93:27). This task will best be performed by individuals and small study groups offering their own conscientious and informed opinion.

Consensus and Criticism

Styles of ecclesiology, such as that of the ARCIC report, that stress the ideal of consensus, of the common mind of the Church, put a premium on constructive criticism and leave little room for controversy over fundamental convictions passionately held. It could even be argued that this kind of approach puts a degree of moral pressure on theologians to conform - not to ask awkward questions and so disturb a virtual unanimity. Yet if conflict over comparatively trivial issues has frequently been the curse of the Church, it is equally true to say that controversy about fundamental questions plays a vital part in the Church's journey into truth. The ecumenical quest presupposes that we take a critical view of our own tradition. As Eugene Fairweather insisted, in the context of the Preparatory Commission for ARCIC: 'true ecumenical dialogue demands commitment to the renewal of our own church life. As long as we take it for granted', he warns, that 'all is for the best in the best of all possible churches - namely, our own' - there is no real hope of coming together. 'It is only when a particular church is ready to cast a critical eye on its own past and present realization of the gospel, as well as on the doctrine and life of other churches, that it can pass from monologue to dialogue' (p. 38). It would be disastrous if, in a Church where the ecumenical process has reached fruition, the scope of criticism were to be curtailed, its voice stifled.

In a paper on authority in the Anglican communion, Stephen Sykes has argued that internal theological criticism is 'intrinsic to the life of the Christian church' and that 'it must learn to worship God and engage in Christian mission at the same time as it argues its way through difficult problems.' It is incumbent on the leaders of the Church, therefore, 'both to give a lead and not to mind contradiction' (1981, pp. 12f). Doctrinal controversy is not a luxury to be tolerated in academics on the fringe of church life, but is present at the heart of 'decisions about the terms of Christian preaching and the style of Christian living' (1978, p. 94).

This is certainly an area where Anglicanism, with its

experience of diversity, tolerance and public discussion with few holds barred, has a contribution to make. As John Macquarrie has observed in *Their Lord and Ours* (ed. M. Santer), the possibility of radical dissent is the mark of a mature, adult society. Anglicanism, for all its faults, exhibits this kind of tolerance and would insist, I hope, on its being safeguarded in any united church. It constitutes an acceptance of the principle - central to the Anglican appeal to sound learning - that a theological question can only be settled by theological work and not by appeal to authority, in the form of either the magisterium or the *consensus fidei*, that would short-cut the process of truth-seeking and enquiry (p. 118).

Within Anglicanism the human means employed in seeking to arrive at the truth - research, debate, criticism - have been openly acknowledged and indeed encouraged. Within the Roman Catholic Church both Karl Rahner and Hans Küng have called for more frank acknowledgement of these fallible but indispensable human means instead of the habit of drawing a veil of mystery over the Church's truth-seeking and decision-making processes.

Rahner has repeatedly made the point - in his characteristically cautious, tentative but insistent way - that the situation in which the Church now finds herself demands that the post-Enlightenment critical approach, pervasive in the modern world, should be incorporated into Christian commitment to the Church. One cannot today be totally committed to the Church without at the same time being involved in a critical relationship to her. Rahner therefore asserts that 'the church's self-understanding and its own faith do not merely permit the Catholic to have an oppositional relationship to the church . . . or make this unavoidable. An attitude of this kind is actually required of us' (XVII, p. 129; cf. XII, pp. 11f). Similarly, Hans Küng, both in his early work *The Council and Reunion* (pp. 61-70) and more recently in *The Church: Maintained in Truth*, has developed his views on the necessity of criticism in the Church, remarking in the latter work that conflicts are signs of life and infinitely preferable to 'the deathly silence of totalitarian systems' (pp. 60f). What Küng has been open about - and got into trouble for it - and Rahner loath to concede, is that to accept the discipline of internal criticism and the principle of reform that it entails presents a radical challenge to the fundamental assumptions of Catholic ecclesiology.

John de Satgé, an Anglican advocate of reunion with Rome without concession on her part - with no strings attached - describes the nature of catholicism with stark candour. Catholic theology is 'essentially cumulative'. 'It is marked by continuity so that nothing which has once been declared true can later be declared false' (p. 64). Another Anglican, Austin Farrer, put it more abrasively (at the same time reminding us of a hard dominical injunction that we would do well to relate to the doctrine of the Church), when he remarked that the Roman Catholic Church 'can never bury its dead' (Goulder, ed., p. 18).

Finally, if, in addition to a greater openness in the Church's doctrinal investigations and moral and pastoral assessments, the realities of power-politics in the counsels and synods of both the Anglican and Roman Catholic Churches were more frankly admitted, the precarious, fragile and contingent character of its possession of truth would become obvious. It would be a salutary development if this led to the abandonment of idealistic talk about 'the mind of the Church' and complacent romanticizing about the Church dwelling in the truth.

Consensus and Comprehensiveness

The Anglican-Roman Catholic International Commission published its *Final Report* shortly before the Pope's historic visit to Britain in the summer of 1982. At this juncture, the Archbishop of Canterbury was asked whether this meant that reunion between Rome and Canterbury was now in sight. Dr Runcie replied that he still remained sceptical of a system in which all the answers came out of the Vatican.

The Archbishop was speaking not only on behalf of a modernity that believes that big is not beautiful and that highly centralized bureaucratic structures like the Vatican (or the

Pentagon, or the Kremlin, for that matter) do not have the intellectual mobility to come up with the right answers and have not been conspicuously successful in doing so. He was also speaking from within an ecclesiastical tradition that embodies the principle of *dispersed authority*, operating by a system of checks and balances - a tradition, moreover, that at the Reformation had welcomed the new learning of Renaissance humanism and had long ago come to terms with the historical, critical and analytical ways of thinking of the Enlightenment, in a way that the Roman Catholic tradition clearly had not.

In the ARCIC report, however, we find that, in the final analysis, all the answers that matter still come out of the Vatican. The statement envisages a universal primate, presiding over a united church as the sign and safeguard of its unity, and endowed with the authority to articulate the mind of the Church on urgent matters of doctrinal, moral or pastoral significance. While the report has certainly diluted the authority of the papal chair by stressing the need for both consultation with the bishops and consent of the faithful, the residual centralized authority is still sufficient to represent - as the report puts it - 'a special ministerial gift of discerning the truth and of teaching bestowed at crucial times on one person to enable him to speak authoritatively in the name of the church in order to preserve the people of God in the truth' (p. 92:23).

There is a particular difficulty for Anglicans here. The Commission points out (p. 95:29) that Anglicans would be obliged to reserve reception of any definition 'not manifestly a legitimate interpretation of biblical faith and in line with orthodox tradition' so that study and discussion could take place (what then?). But this is not the only or the chief problem. It is more relevant to ask whether this scenario, which involves entrusting a single authority with responsibility for articulating the mind of the Church, is compatible - not merely with the Anglican machinery of discussion and decision - but with the spirit or ethos of Anglicanism as such. Is it congenial to the Anglican approach, involving as it does a dispersed authority, without a central focus, working by a system of checks and balances? (The allusion to the democratic constitutions, with their separation of powers, guardians of a liberal society, without positive collectivist aims and keeping interference with the freedoms of the individual to a minimum, is not accidental.) The world-wide Anglican Communion would rightly be suspicious of any centralization of authority invested in a single individual that went beyond the kind of personal, moral and pastoral leadership now exercised by the Archbishop of Canterbury.

The ideal of an ecumenical consensus extending to specific points of doctrine, ethics or pastoral practice seems unrealistic in the face of the endemic pluralism within the churches. It might, however, be dismissed as harmless romanticizing, if it were not for the fact that it affects a fundamental principle of religious liberty. Anglican comprehensiveness permits a latitude of belief and practice on inessentials within a common discipline of worship and pastoral structure in the parish system. Many Anglicans see this not as a weakness to be cured by a more powerful influence of the whole over the parts, but as a valid model of coexistence in the Church, the product of centuries of living, praying – and arguing – within one spiritual family. Anglican comprehensiveness, for all its flaws, might prove to be a pilot scheme for a future united church in which diversity is not only tolerated but welcomed. It is questionable whether the Pope's authority to issue decisions that – whatever the safeguards that the report attempts to build in – are ultimately to be regarded as preserved from error and binding on the whole united church, is compatible with the liberty of individual conscience, of the duty of private judgement, that is intrinsic to Anglicanism.

The binding decisions envisaged by the report will be concerned with matters of either faith or morals. If matters of faith, they will necessarily deal with vexed questions of theological interpretation, since there is agreement on all sides that the Church has no power to invent new articles of faith, *credenda*. But many will doubt whether the papacy is likely to come down invariably on the right side in a theological argument, even after full consultation and the emergence of a consensus – not through any lack of good intentions, but because this very process would inevitably have the effect of stifling minority reforming movements who might well have a prophetic message for the Church.

If, on the other hand, a question of morals were involved, the danger of infringing individual conscience would be more acute. Recent experience suggests that any such ruling on a matter disputed within the Church would generate renewed controversy and would be largely ignored by those put in the wrong, the authority of the magisterium would be undermined and, altogether, the last state would be worse than the first. However, if a 'binding' decision means that conformity would be induced by ecclesiastical sanctions (this is an aspect that the Commission wisely steered clear of, though the cases of Küng and Schillebeeckx make it highly relevant), we would be in a very different situation, for enforced conformity is an experience that few Anglicans – or Roman Catholics, I suspect – would want to repeat.

'The Church of England above all others,' writes John McManners in his valuable contribution to *Believing in the Church*, 'lives by consensus'. Yet it is not a consensus that consists in the unanimity of all church members, nor one that can be identified by reference to the decisions of authority, dutifully embraced by the faithful. It is not specific. You cannot take its temperature. It exists 'in the tacit dimension', as an unwritten understanding between members of a common fellowship, 'a basis for common discussion, exchange of spiritual insights, reflections on our past and common propaganda to the world outside, constituting a base from which the individual can operate, a sign of our unity in love, a recalling of the overwhelming allegiance which dominates our horizon and unites us, a conscious self-defence against the uncomprehending world' (pp. 225f).

The *consensus fidei* is, as Owen Chadwick puts it in expounding Newman, 'that profound understanding, hardly expressed in words, which is the church's immediate apprehension of the Christian way of life' (p. 42). We cannot easily know what the mind of the Church is thinking, and it may not be constructive to attempt to find out, but we can be sure that its heart is in the right place!

5

Pluralism and Prophecy

One of the most conspicuous attributes of modern theology is its preoccupation with the problems raised by the acknowledged pluralism of the modern world. We are acutely aware that the phenomenon of pluralism raises questions for traditional theology to which adequate answers are not yet available. While the ARCIC documents recognize that this situation exists, it must be said that they do not allow it to influence their conclusions with regard to the Church's teaching office.

The problem of cultural pluralism began to make itself felt as the result of two factors: the assimilation of new facts about other races and cultures discovered during the great voyages of exploration in the fifteenth and sixteenth centuries, and the rise of the historical movement with its inductive and comparative method, entailing the redating and reconstruction of documents, critical analysis of supposed eye-witness accounts and a characteristic refusal to be bound by traditional interpretations. Modern philosophy and hermeneutics have emphasized the difficulty of translating the ideas and assumptions of one age into those of another. Historical relativism (or *diachronic* pluralism) presents an obvious challenge to the work of reformulating Christian doctrine in every age and relating it to the foundation documents of Christianity.

At the same time, we have been made uncomfortably aware of the phenomenon of cultural relativism (or *synchronic* pluralism) which calls in question the possibility of understanding the other person's point of view. The mass media, extensive travel and tourism, mass literacy and wholesale immigration have made cultural diversity a reality for many people. While supra-national influences like 'Americanization',

82

Marxist ideology, the United Nations agencies and the multi-national business corporations may moderate the starker aspects of cultural diversity, they only scratch the surface. While this has obvious consequences for the Church's apologetic and evangelistic mission, we are concerned here with what it implies for its ecumenical task.

The Second Vatican Council gave its blessing to the principle of pluralism within the world Church, acknowledging that the Catholic faith will take diverse forms in different cultures (V2, p. 306). But it did not tackle the question, that has so exercised Catholic theologians such as Rahner, of how this pluralism is to be reconciled with the unity of the Church and the authority of the Pope (XIV, p. 119). Both Rahner and Lonergan see in the phenomenon of pluralism a radical new challenge to Christian theology, but neither of them laments this fact or reluctantly attempts to cope with it as merely a necessary evil. Lonergan's analysis of the situation is that we have moved from a *classical* (normative, uniformitarian) understanding of culture to an *empirical* (pluralist) notion of culture in which our particular set of assumptions about life is merely one option among many. In this context theology, no longer the queen of the sciences, has an interpretative role, mediating between a specific culture and the role of religion in that culture, or, to put it a slightly different way, reflecting on the significance of a religion in a culture. Obviously, theology is no longer a 'system valid for all times and places' but is 'as manifold as are the many cultures within which a religion has significance and value' (1973, pp. 33f).

This chronic pluralism is compounded by another factor: what Lonergan calls our *polymorphic consciousness* – the fact that our minds are subject to many impulses and influences that mediate the pure desire to know that Lonergan postulates at the heart of human nature. (Needless to say, Lonergan is not content to leave it there. He believes that his cognitional theory transcends cultural diversity and that his method can attain the truth in every culture-bound version of religious faith.)

The declaration *Mysterium Ecclesiae* acknowledged the fact that dogmas are historically conditioned. John de Satgé takes this as the charter for critical scrutiny of all dogmatic pronouncements of the magisterium, as though it had the effect of relativizing the very notion of dogma itself (p. 123f). But this was certainly not the intention of the declaration, which makes it clear that historical conditioning does not impair the truth of dogma. It only implies that it is susceptible to a later process of perfection. 'It sometimes happens that some dogmatic truth is first expressed incompletely (but not falsely), and at a later date, when considered in a broader context of faith or human knowledge, it receives a fuller and more perfect expression.' The declaration asserts, moreover, that the Church can distinguish the timeless essence of truth from its diverse historical expression and even enunciate it in terms that transcend a specific time and place. The Church's truth can be expressed independently of the culture-specific meanings of the time (DC, p. 60). This view will be greeted with extreme scepticism both within and without the Roman Catholic Church and has been explicitly challenged by Karl Rahner (XVII, p. 152).

Anglicanism is no stranger to questions of pluralism, which go back to its historical origins in the sixteenth century. A synthesis was attempted in the heat of controversy and under the pressure of political upheaval, where an appeal to the fathers of the undivided primitive Church was combined with the stimulating humanism of the Renaissance and acceptance of the fundamental positions of the Continental Reformers. The tensions thus engendered were contained by the relative continuity of the parochial ministry and by the political imposition of outward uniformity. As a result, Anglicanism has an inbuilt pluralism, an inherent openness to diverse sources of theological reflection. It draws together various threads of understanding and insight, and trusts that out of the tensions that result some broadly based synthesis may emerge. Exponents of Anglicanism have held it out as an attempt to combine elements which in other traditions have become sundered.

It is true to say, however, that this synthesis has only been attained by Anglicanism's most creative and irenic theologians

- Hooker in the sixteenth century, Maurice in the nineteenth, and Charles Gore and Michael Ramsey in the twentieth. For the most part, her pluralism has taken the form of a complacent comprehensiveness in which there was little attempt to reconcile conflicting views. Stephen Sykes' timely tract *The Integrity of Anglicanism* has compelled re-examination of this issue, while the Church of England's Doctrine Commissions have also given it their attention in a series of reports. *Doctrine in the Church of England* (1938) is an urbane and uninspiring committee-production that conveys the impression that Christian doctrine is nothing to get excited about and the Church of England has no intention of doing so. As a study of diversity within Anglicanism, the report is extraordinary in that it neither mentions justification (for Protestants the crux of true doctrine, *articulus stantis aut cadentis ecclesiae*) nor discusses the meaning of faith. Yet it has value in setting out the scope of acceptable doctrinal diversity in the Church of England.

The publication *Christian Believing* (1976) gave for the first time a quasi-official platform to Anglican theologians to voice their doubts and difficulties concerning historical relativism, though without making constructive proposals as to how a confessional church should respond to this new situation. *Believing in the Church* (1981), the work of a fresh commission, was intended to have a reassuring effect. Though including much valuable material in its individual essays, it made no attempt at an agreed statement and did not attempt to tackle the questions that pluralism raises for theological *method*.

The ARCIC documents recognize the reality of historical and cultural pluralism, acknowledging that 'the Church's life and work are shaped by its historical origins, by its subsequent experience, and by its endeavour to make the relevance of the gospel plain to every generation.' It affirms that 'all generations and cultures must be helped to understand that the good news of salvation is also for them.' Consequently, 'it is not enough for the Church simply to repeat the original apostolic words. It has also prophetically to translate them in order that the hearers in their situation may understand and respond to

85

them.' The report also acknowledges that the authoritative definitions of the magisterium 'are provoked by specific historical situations and are always made in terms of the understanding and framework of their age' (pp. 59:15, 93:27).

This has clear implications for our understanding of development in relation to the indefectibility of the Church, since it suggests that several - perhaps numerous - lines of development will be taking place at any one time throughout the world-wide Church - a consideration that is bound to affect the scope and status of central magisterial pronouncements. While the ARCIC statements do not appear to take account of this problem, we shall return to it in the chapter on the indefectibility of the Church. Meanwhile, let us turn now to the state of pluralism *between* the churches and what this entails for the task of ecumenical theology.

The External Forum

We are by now familiar with the notion of a plurality of theologies within both the Old and New Testaments, brought to light by the research of biblical scholars. The plurality of theologies within the New Testament has given rise to a plurality of traditions in the Church as various strands within the New Testament lent themselves to adoption into a particular cultural milieu with distinctive philosophical assumptions and conceptual apparatus.

Thus the Greek church became Johannine and Platonic; the Latin church combined the themes of the catholic epistles and the more ecclesiastical aspects of St Paul with elements of the Stoic philosophical tradition such as natural law, and subsequently reformulated its doctrine within an Aristotelian conceptual framework. The Western church in the middle ages contained its pluralistic tendencies by its common language and philosophical tradition and by a monarchical papacy. But that synthesis was dissolved by the combined action of the humanist Renaissance, the Protestant Reformation and the rise of the nation state. The Reformed churches became basically Pauline and Aristotelian in theological method, while the Anglican

Church has experienced the tension of Platonic and Aristotelian modes of thought.

The diversity of traditions is complicated today by other factors that cut across confessional divisions. In the process of theological development, further diversity is created by the various philosophical and methodological assumptions of individual theologians. If, for example, like Barth you believe that metaphysical thinking is an intrusion on the theological scene, you will come up with a very different theology to that of say Rahner, who employs a method that is speculative rather than exegetical, or the Anglican philosophical theologian F.R. Tennant who, working in the tradition of Joseph Butler, held that all theological issues must be subjected to rigorous philosophical scrutiny.

Dialogue between Christian theology and the physical or social sciences, other world religions or ideologies, such as Marxism, and attempts to meet new challenges such as secularization, will lead to a shift of emphasis at the very least, and the translation of concepts into a new idiom. The central affirmations of Christian theology will not remain untouched.

Furthermore, the progressively greater sophistication of theological procedures leads inevitably to greater specialization, with the result that, as Schillebeeckx says, 'a theologian, or even a group of theologians working together, has no more than a limited and one-sided view of the totality of the reality of faith.' 'Because of this,' he concludes, 'no theologian can say that what he does not see is theologically irrelevant or even less important than what he has himself discovered' (p. 51).

The churches have always had to grapple with the question of what separated them from their sister churches and on what legitimate grounds they could take their stand *vis à vis* other ecclesial bodies. Superficially they may appear to take up positions on such issues as church government, infant versus adult baptism, adherence to the doctrinal standards laid down by Luther, Wesley or the Westminster divines, or the primacy of the Bishop of Rome.

Beneath the surface, however, these ostensibly theological criteria may recede in importance and factors deriving from historical accident, political involvement, social interests, and the culture-specific development of different styles of worship and diverse languages of Christian experience loom larger. To bring these underlying issues into the open, to subject them to critical analysis and to assess their continuing validity is the proper task of ecumenical theology in collaboration with the social study of religion.

Each church must be helped to take a disapassionate and critical look at those commitments that constitute its ecclesial identity. Each church must ask itself whether those things that are so deeply embedded in its tradition are mere accidents of history, the precipitate of cultural changes, or whether, on the other hand, they are actually grounded on the one and only foundation of the Christian Church – the nature of God, the person of Christ and the character of the Christian gospel (1 Cor. 3.11). This could well form the subject of another ecumenical commission, with a significant sociological component, whose task would be complementary to the purely doctrinal work of ARCIC.

Internal Ecumenism

This question of ecclesial identity in the *external* forum, that is to say, in relation to other churches, which constitutes one of the primary tasks of ecumenical theology, has its counterpart in the question of ecclesial identity in the *internal* forum, that is to say, with regard to a given church's own internal unity, its ecclesiological integrity. In the external forum, the problem of ecclesial identity is the problem of the plurality of churches; in the internal forum, the problem of ecclesial identity is the problem of pluralism within a church. The issue is that of unity in diversity. The diversity of doctrinal views, and in some cases, liturgical practices and ethical norms (birth-control, political involvement, pacifism) represented within the main Christian traditions raises acutely the problem of their integration as churches.

Just as every church needs to take a critical look at its ecclesial identity *vis à vis* other churches (the external forum), so too every church must take heed to its internal integrity (the internal forum). Both ecumenical considerations, as to where a particular church stands on a particular matter, and reflection on theological method, with its alertness to the hidden methodological axioms, good and bad, that underlie all theology, demand that this question receive the attention of the churches' councils and that its implications for the ecumenical process be assessed.

In 'Pluralism in Theology and the Unity of the Creed in the Church', Karl Rahner has expressed an extremely pessimistic view about the possibilities for meaningful communication within the Church. 'Formerly,' he observes, 'it was possible to proceed from the basic principle that one could know the position of one's opponent. One could understand it and could oneself explain to him why one could not share it.' Both parties had a terminology and set of philosophical presuppositions in common; differences of underlying attitude and feeling were not brought out into the open. But now, Rahner claims, we have arrived at a situation where 'the representatives of the different schools cannot achieve, even indirectly, a position in which they can explain to one another consciously and unambiguously in what precisely the difference between their respective intellectual outlooks consists' (XI, pp. 3–23).

Rahner's words are a despairing reflection on the ferment within contemporary Roman Catholicism world-wide. The problem that he describes could only become exacerbated (if that were possible) in a united Church into which other traditions – each containing their own diversity – had been incorporated. Yet this whole dimension of pluralism within the churches is ignored by the ARCIC statement, though the fact of pluralism undermines the assumptions of the report that it is possible for the Church to come to a common mind and feasible for its teaching authority to make decisions that are both relevant to the situation and universally binding, let alone free from error.

The Prophetic Office

It is the official teaching of the Roman Catholic Church that its definitions of doctrine are not dependent on any particular school of thought, but are autonomous, being divinely assisted, and are capable of being expressed in a form independent of the thought-forms of the time (DC, p. 60). Karl Rahner has asserted, however, that, on the contrary, the teaching authority of the Church can only operate in dependence on a particular theology. His view is now likely to receive widespread, if not unanimous, agreement. Today there exists a plurality of theologies, each of which employs - and is acknowledged to employ - methods and concepts that are historically and culturally conditioned. Because they are specific to a particular culture they cannot be absolutized by being embodied in the dogmatic decisions of the magisterium (XI, p. 19).

Rahner's thesis gains support from the discipline of the sociology of religion. As Max Weber showed, religious bodies tend to fall into one of two archetypes, the priestly or the prophetic. A society that is by nature priestly, as the Church evidently is, cannot at the same time be prophetic. It is inevitably concerned with upholding a given rite and maintaining orthodoxy. Furthermore, the degree of social and cultural determinism is vastly greater in the case of a community than in the case of the individual prophetic or priestly figure. These considerations might well lead us to conclude that the Church as a whole is not equipped for a prophetic role, can rarely speak with a single voice and must rely for the fulfilment of its prophetic office on individual prophetic voices from its midst proclaiming the truth as they see it.

Let me now try to spell out some of the specific implications of this state of ecclesial pluralism for the Church's teaching office. First, we can be quite clear that, generally speaking, the capacity of the magisterium to issue authoritative teachings will be drastically curtailed. As Rahner puts it, 'In the future the magisterium will hardly be in a position to arrive at any fresh positive expressions of doctrine' (XI, p. 19). Rahner clearly implies that the pronouncements of the Church will be rendered both trivial and ineffectual.

Second, the process of the development of officially sanctioned doctrine may be said to have come to an end, since as we have already observed, in a pluralistic Church there will be not one, but many separate lines of development taking place. Rahner therefore advocates 'the relinquishment of a "development of dogma"', and argues that what is required instead of the elaboration of dogma is a process of increasing *rapport* between the Christian gospel and the various cultural settings into which it is projected. The future of doctrine in the Church, he claims, will tend not towards 'further material differentiation of the substance of the Christian faith, but towards a new expression of the ultimate basic substance of Christianity, corresponding to the mental climate and socio-political situation of today and tomorrow.' And the dream of some theologians of a process of ever more refined development of dogma, will prove to be groundless (XI, pp. 19f; XX, p. 139).

Third, the binding authority of such pronouncements as the centralized magisterium feels able to make is bound to be severely curtailed, since they will be seen to embody a partial point of view, dependent on one school or style of theology among many. The claim to issue decisions that are universally binding, still envisaged by the ARCIC statements (p. 95:29) is therefore based on an illusion.

Fourth, theologians, working individually or in teams, will enjoy an enhanced autonomy. As Rahner points out, whereas the central theses of earlier theologies were perforce borrowed from the definitions of the magisterium, in future these theologies will address themselves to the most fundamental questions of the Christian faith in their own way and apply them to contemporary issues. 'The most central and most radical points in the content of the Christian faith will be considered, interpreted and applied to the present by theologies which are, and will continue to be, very different in character' (XI, p. 20). We therefore foresee a prophetic role for individual theologians rather than for a central teaching authority in the form envisaged by the ARCIC statement.

Finally, any such pronouncements as the magisterium should venture to make will be frankly trivial in content. As an attempt to arrive at definitions that do not reflect a particular contested point of view in a pluralistic Church, but can command wide acceptance, they will remain at the level of platitudes. We have already made this point in connection with the notion of consensus, but it arises again in the context of pluralism. Let me illustrate the point by reference to Peter Chirico's presentation of infallibility.

Chirico is enabled to defend the notion of infallibility by restricting it drastically. He confines infallible truth to universal statements, either of faith or morals: 'The truths of faith are the universal . . . aspects of revelation; . . . the truths of morals are the recurring dynamic principles which characterize the growth of men in all cultures and times' (p. 193). In other words, the definitions of the magisterium that are to be regarded as authoritative, binding and inerrant will be abstract rather than concrete, general rather than particular, dogmatic rather than prophetic.

Chirico points out that the higher one goes in the hierarchy, the more universal the pronouncements should be if they are to act as a unifying influence in the Church. He observes that in the early Church it was possible for the highest authority in the Church (the Council of Jerusalem, for example: Acts 15) to issue decisions that were immediately applicable to concrete situations. The Church could exercise its prophetical office without the constraints imposed by a pluralistic constituency. But a modern Pope, whose task is to unify a Church characterized by extreme diversity, can no longer articulate the truth for concrete situations in an authoritative way. He can only enunciate abstract, universal truths that belong to the whole Church (pp. 217f; 63; 197). As Chirico presents it, the papacy would become the mouthpiece of platitudes uttered with ludicrously disproportionate solemnity.

This restriction excludes precisely those areas where Christians and non-Christians look to the Church to give a lead – sexual ethics, including birth control and abortion, and issues of war and peace, including the nuclear question. This leads

Chirico to ask whether the power to define infallibly has any practical value, since it contributes little towards settling the concrete problems that the Church faces in its encounter with the modern world. These are not the objects of infallible decisions (pp. 186, 199).

Chirico's work, a sophisticated and sustained reinterpretation of infallibility, which sets out to give a new lease of life to a doctrine originally defined in the uniformitarian concepts that modern awareness of pluralism has superseded, ultimately has the opposite effect. Specifically, it undermines the confidence of the ARCIC report that the papacy in a united Church would effectively apply Christian principles to contemporary issues.

6

Stages on the Journey into Truth

The Church, wrote St Augustine in Book XVIII of *The City of God*, 'like a pilgrim in a foreign land, presses forward amid the persecutions of the world and the consolations of God' (XVIII, p. 51). The Second Vatican Council cites this passage and continually invokes the image of the wayfaring people of God. By adopting the theme of the pilgrim Church as its watchword, the Council changed the tone of Roman Catholic ecclesiology, forswore triumphalism, and made common cause with the Protestant notion of the Church undergoing continual reform (*ecclesia semper reformanda*).

Or did it?

What does it imply when the Council asserts: 'The bride of the incarnate Word, and the pupil of the Holy Spirit, the church is concerned to move ahead daily toward a deeper understanding of the sacred scriptures'? And what sort of ecclesiology – that of a *theologia crucis* or that of a *theologia gloriae* – underlies this declaration: 'As the centuries succeed one another, the church constantly moves forward toward the fulness of divine truth until the words of God reach their complete fulfilment in her' (V2, pp. 126, 116)?

These claims of Vatican II, that the Church progresses in her grasp of the truth, that she sees it more clearly now than she did before, will evoke a very wary response from Anglicans. Whatever else the Church of England may or may not owe to the Oxford Movement, she has absorbed into her way of thinking the inseparable connection that the Tractarians (and before them, the seventeenth-century divines) made between truth and holiness. Anglicanism has adopted the principle that growth in holiness is a precondition for growth in the knowledge of God. It follows that we could only subscribe to

es as concerned with points in dispute; it is not evidence
he Church of England does not hold the indefectibility of
hurch.

s, however, when we come to the question of what is
ed from the fundamental indefectibility of the Church
ve reach the parting of the ways between Catholic and
tant ecclesiology. They do not draw the same con-
ns. As we have already seen, for ARCIC, indefectibility is
esupposition on which a notion of an inerrant teaching
embodied in councils or the universal primate, is
ucted. For Rahner too, the indefectibility of faith and the
unity of faith imply the indefectibility of the propositions
ch this faith is expressed, and it is necessary that some of
hould be 'infallible and inerrant propositions' (XIV, p.
r the Reformers, on the other hand (as for Hans Küng
course), indefectibility entails no such consequences.
em, there are no limits to how far the fallibility of the
may extend – except one: it can never finally lose the
e of salvation, the gospel.

English Reformers affirm in no uncertain terms the
tibility of the Church. There will always be a Church, for
will never forsake his bride and has promised that the
hell shall not prevail. This indefectibility consists in the
at the Church will never finally depart from the gospel,
th of salvation. As far as saving doctrine is concerned,
Bullinger, 'the church of Christ doth not err. For it
the voice of the Shepherd only, but the voice of
rs she knoweth not.' Churches cannot 'err damnably',
yndale, 'nor any long time, nor all of them', and
ing needful to salvation will be taught. But notwith-
g this ultimate fidelity to the gospel, serious error may
spread and even prevalent in the Church. The greater
the universal Church and the whole of any particular
may forsake faith, depart from the true worship of God
to follow the word of God.

English Reformers postulate a Church that, as far as its
spiritual reality as the body of Christ is concerned,
n the truth of the gospel, but as far as its outward

the picture presented in Vatican II of the Church making progress in its grasp of the truth and advancing in the knowledge of God, if it could be claimed that the Church of today surpassed the Church of yesterday in the love of God and obedience to his will.

The Church's journey into truth is an eschatological image. It is not empirically cashable. To borrow a phrase from Newman, it involves loss as well as gain, regress as well as progress. Models of development that suggest that the Church can rise on stepping stones of its past self to higher things - by analogy of the acorn and the oak, the child and the adult - need to be used with caution. They are not the invention of nineteenth-century theorists of development like Newman, but the time-worn stock-in-trade of Roman Catholic self-justificatory polemic. In the sixteenth century Bishop Jewel had to counter the claim that the Tridentine Catholic Church represented the mature development of infant apostolic Christianity. Who are you, he asked, to make yourselves fathers of the Church and to imply that the apostles were babes in Christ?

Vatican II's picture of the spreading dawn of enlightenment by divine truth within the Church perhaps owes more to modern (and discredited) notions of inevitable progress than to the biblical images of the journey of faith. Hans Küng is closer to the spirit of biblical Christianity when he compares the Church to the people of Israel on their far from glorious progress to the promised land, to the Prodigal Son in a far country, to the lost sheep on the mountainside, or to the man who fell among thieves on the way to Jericho:

> The church goes on its pilgrim way through the ages, along a road not of its choosing, along the way to which it is irrevocably called. It may lose the way, make detours, take wrong turnings, it may stumble and fall, it may fall among thieves and lie half-dead by the roadside. But God the Lord will not pass by on the other side; he will pour oil on its wounds, lift it up, give it a lodging and provide for its healing (1971b, p. 344).

The Fallible Church

'Indefectibility' is a word to conjure with in modern ecclesiology. It represents an attempt to find common ground between Catholic and Protestant understandings of the Church. For progressive Catholics, like Küng, it serves as a substitute for infallibility and demonstrates an intention to remain faithful to the spirit of Catholic ecclesiology. For mediating Catholic theologians, like Rahner, it serves as a sort of smoke-screen behind which a sophisticated concept of infallibility can be deployed. For conservative Catholics, like Ratzinger, it is to be viewed with suspicion as the thin end of the wedge, concealing an abandonment of the Catholic doctrine of the teaching office of the Church. As the *Observations* of the SCDF point out, the ARCIC report uses the term in a different, reductionist sense compared with that intended by Vatican I.

ARCIC's first statement on authority (1976) contained a somewhat subdued affirmation of the indefectibility of the Church. Though there is no guarantee, the statement conceded, that those who bear office in the Church will invariably be free from error, always conscientiously reform abuses and never distort the truth, yet, it went on, 'in Christian hope we are confident that such failures cannot destroy the church's ability to proclaim the gospel and to show forth the Christian life; for we believe that Christ will not desert his Church and that the Holy Spirit will lead it into all truth' (p. 62:8).

But the statement also contains a stronger version of indefectibility, that is not so much an expression of faith in the ultimate faithfulness of God to his people, as a celebration of the unconditional, empirically verifiable perfection of the Church *as it now is*.

> The Spirit of the risen Lord, who indwells the Christian community, continues to maintain the people of God in obedience to the Father's will. He safeguards their faithfulness to the revelation of Jesus Christ and equips them for their mission in the world. By this action of the Holy Spirit the authority of the Lord is active in the Church (p. 53:3).

There is an obvious problem about i statement into ecumenical discussion b disagree over many important matters Church is now in possession of the t fulfilling her divine calling in implicit o God. But when there exist serious dif churches, it is impossible to predicate t the truth of them all – or, in the case o them both. The question therefore aris *this being said?* The answer must be, o case, it undermines the grounds for between the two parties.

Perhaps that is why the *Final Report* the Church II' (1981) reverts mere Church's confidence that she will not b mission. Furthermore this confidence i her fidelity to the truth as it is made kn Church . . . is witness, teacher and gu confident that the Holy Spirit will effec its mission so that it will neither lose its fail to reach its goal' (p. 91:23).

It is worth comparing this cautious v with the way that Karl Rahner has rein For Rahner, the proper starting-point is the revelation of God: faith in his a 'something which henceforth can never indestructibility of this faith is itself an of the faith. But faith cannot exist in a in persons who constitute a community Jesus Christ also implies faith in the sur faith gathered about Jesus Christ, which bears witness to this indestructible fait pp. 112f). Here there is genuine comm Catholic and Protestant traditions. Th declares that 'one holy Christian Churc ever' and Reformed theology endorses indefectibility of the Church is not affi Articles of the Church of England refl

political aspect is concerned, holds this truth in earthen vessels. The Reformers knew only too well how fragile the Church's tenure of truth is, what efforts have to be made to preserve it, and what a price has sometimes to be paid to do so.

For the Reformers, indefectibility is like walking a tightrope with infallibility on one side and apostasy on the other. Underlying this somewhat paradoxical concept of indefectibility is their conviction that the Church's faithfulness to the truth is not dependent on the hierarchy but dwells in the body of the faithful - if necessary in an elect remnant. Here they are following Luther and Calvin, who are unimpressed by the claim of their opponents that the Church's hierarchy and general councils are the only reliable guardians of the truth. Our faith, asserts Cranmer, does not rest on 'the outward, glistering and pompous church' comprising the succession of bishops, 'in such pompous and glorious sort as now is seen'. And Philpot, at his examination by Bonner, made it clear that while he embraced the doctrine of the indefectibility of the Church, he did not regard this as inhering in the Church of Rome and its hierarchy: 'I do not think that the catholic church can err in doctrine; but I require you to prove this church of Rome to be the catholic church.'

Just as the Reformers clung to the hope that the divisions of Christendom might be healed by a great council at which their case would be heard without prejudice, so today Roman Catholics and Anglicans are resting their hopes of ecumenical agreement to a large extent on the notion of the ecumenical council. By making great play of the concept of a council, the Catholics can satisfy the demands of their tradition for a decisive teaching office and Anglicans can do justice to their notion of dispersed authority.

The starting point of the ARCIC documents on the question of councils is found in the Church's mission to proclaim and safeguard the gospel. To enable her to carry out this divine commission, she has the duty and the ability to make declarations in matters of faith. Though it is no part of her teaching ministry to add new truths of revelation, in times of crisis or when fundamental matters of faith are in question, the

Church can make doctrinal judgements, consonant with Scripture, formulating the central truths of salvation and therefore authoritative and binding. The purpose of these judgements, the report confidently explains, is 'to recall and emphasize some important truth; to expound the faith more lucidly; to expose error; to draw out implications not sufficiently recognized; and to show how Christian truth applies to contemporary issues' (p. 93:27).

While we might want to question the feasibility of carrying out this mandate to the letter in today's pluralistic situation, there is nothing here that is incompatible in principle with Anglicanism. Article XX states that the Church has 'authority in controversies of faith' and, as we have already seen, this is endorsed by the English Reformers. The ARCIC report, however, in common with Roman Catholic ecclesiology, holds that to fulfil this mandate of teaching the truth and giving judgement in questions of doctrine, there must be some guarantee of divine assistance which will prevent the Church from falling into error when it meets together in an ecumenical council to decide disputed matters of fundamental doctrine. Through the council or the Pope in his role as the mouthpiece of the teaching Church, the Church can make decisive judgements in matters of faith and, provided its decisions are 'faithful to scripture' and 'consistent with tradition', they will be protected from error (p. 62:19).

However, one can only marvel at the naivety of the assumption that the phrases 'faithful to scripture' and 'consistent with tradition', stated without qualification, actually mean anything in this context, and at the glibness with which the complex issues involved in the hermeneutics of Scripture and tradition are glossed over and the historical conflicts and controversies over what was in fact faithful to Scripture and consistent with tradition are ignored. Is it unreasonable to ask what basis there is in the Anglican tradition for this notion of an inerrant defining authority in the Church? This question touches on the reformed character of the Church of England.

Jaroslav Pelikan has pointed out that it was Luther's

admission at the Leipzig Disputation of 1519 that general councils can err which constituted the crucial initiation of the Reformation as a separate theological movement (p. 54). The Thirty-Nine Articles not only state that councils may err and actually have erred, but seem to anticipate the elusive notion of inerrancy to be found in the ARCIC report when they assert that they have erred 'even in things pertaining unto God' (1571); or as the Latin text of 1563 puts it, things pertaining to the rule of faith (*etiam in hijs quae ad normam pietatis pertinent*). Similarly, Article XIX states that 'the church of Rome hath erred, not only in their living and manner of ceremonies, but also in matters of faith.'

In the period of its formation, Anglicanism did not accept that the decisions of councils were underwritten in any way by the promises of God or the presiding influence of the Holy Spirit. Field does not believe that they have special divine assistance, though their decisions merit a presumption of truth. Jeremy Taylor comments that the Church of England receives the first four general councils 'as of highest regard, not that they are infallible, but that they have determined wisely and holily'. Burnet remarks that 'we reverence those councils for the sake of their doctrine; but we do not believe the doctrine for the authority of the councils'.

William Laud comes closest to the qualified view of conciliar inerrancy put forward in the ARCIC statements. Laud painstakingly develops the position that general councils, fully representative of the whole Church (this excluded all councils since the separation of East and West, not to mention the Reformation), submitting itself to the teaching of the Holy Spirit 'in the scripture' (this excludes tradition as a source of doctrine) cannot err in matters necessary to salvation – for the simple reason that the Church as a whole cannot lose the truth of salvation and the council as Laud envisages it is merely stating the mind of the Church, not deciding on questions that are the subject of dispute within the Church.

The Tractarians, though obviously abandoning the Protestant principle of *sola scriptura*, retain the safeguards insisted on by Laud, thus falling far short of the Roman Catholic understanding of tradition and councils. William Palmer, for example, in his great treatise on the Church, asserts that 'any doctrine established by universal tradition' must be 'divinely, infallibly, true' since 'it rests on evidence not inferior to that which attests the truth of Christianity.' But the function of this universal, undisputed tradition is to be confirmatory of Scripture and to serve as a guide to its interpretation, not, Palmer points out, to convey doctrines not found in Scripture, as in 'the popular Romish doctrine of tradition'. In this task, councils stand alongside creeds, liturgies, customs and rites, and the writings of the fathers as one witness among many (II, pp. 33-36).

There is nothing in the Anglican tradition that would provide a point of contact with the teaching of the Second Vatican Council that the college of bishops, convened in council, presided over and confirmed by the Pope, is *ipso facto* infallible (V2, pp. 44, 48). The Anglican position, in regarding councils as the mouthpiece of a Church which cannot lose the knowledge of salvation, seems to approximate closer to the Orthodox view, according to which infallibility resides in the whole Church and can be predicated of councils simply because their voice is the voice of the Church, than to the Roman Catholic view.

On this understanding, the role of councils is severely restricted. They may serve as a platform for the Church to declare its fundamental faith to the world or to itself in times of perplexity. But its declarations (as we already see in the communiqués of synods, etc.) will necessarily be truisms; they will have to consist of self-evident truths; they will not solve anything. It is wishful thinking to suppose, as ARCIC does, that ecumenical councils will be able to tackle aberrations of faith or lay down the one Christian response to controversial questions. That is not to say that they should never venture into disputed territory, only that when they do, there are no grounds for supposing that they will reach a common mind or that their findings could be published as representing the mind of the Church. The more contentious the issue, the more divided a council will be and the less authoritative its pronouncements.

Primacy and Providence

A new sense of realism and purposefulness in the ecumenical quest was signalled in 1967 when Pope Paul VI confessed that the papacy itself was 'undoubtedly the gravest obstacle in the path of ecumenism'. The Second Vatican Council, which had recently concluded its deliberations, had certainly done little to ease the difficulties felt by other churches over the question of papal primacy, though it goes without saying that, by its irenical tone and its evident status as the manifesto of a reforming church, it had done a great deal to improve the atmosphere of inter-church relations.

The Second Vatican Council continued to appeal to the dominical institution both of Peter as head of the 'apostolic college' and of a permanent Petrine office in the Church. Christ 'placed blessed Peter over the other apostles, and instituted in him a permanent and visible source and foundation of unity of faith and fellowship' (V2, p. 38). Vatican II went out of its way to endorse the teaching of *Pastor aeternus* of Vatican I concerning 'the institution, the perpetuity, the force and reason for the sacred primacy of the Roman pontiff and of his infallible teaching authority' which must be 'firmly believed by all the faithful.'

Just as the office of Peter is permanent and 'meant to be transmitted to his successors', so also the office of the apostles is permanent and 'meant to be exercised without interruption by the sacred order of bishops' (V2, p. 40). But the functions of the episcopal college in no way detract from the unrestricted, plenary, supreme and universal authority of the Pope as vicar of Christ and pastor of the whole Church (V2, p. 43). This unqualified reassertion of papal primacy makes no concession to the objections of non-Roman churches and provides little scope for reinterpretation in the cause of ecumenical progress.

If the Anglican–Roman Catholic conversations were not to founder on this 'rock' of papal absolutism, some other point of departure had to be found for discussion of the question of primacy. The ARCIC document therefore boldly abandons any claim that the New Testament and patristic theology provide a firm basis for papal primacy (p. 83:6), and instead appeals to the historical phenomenon of the emergence of the primacy of Rome and its bishop in the providence of God. It reinterprets the *jure divino* language of Vatican I to mean 'at least' that the Roman primacy manifests God's purpose for the Church (p. 86:11). It expresses the hope that it might be possible for the Anglican churches to come to recognize the development of the Roman primacy as 'a gift of divine providence . . . an effect of the guidance of the Holy Spirit in the church – part of God's design for the universal *koinonia*' (pp. 87:13, 88:15).

At first sight this might seem to be a commendable approach. The principle of primacy evidently not being negotiable on the Roman Catholic side, and critical study of the New Testament providing a shaky foundation for appeals to dominical institution, the basis of primacy has been shifted from the realm of the empirically verifiable or refutable to the realm of faith. Whether or not a particular development in history can be attributed to the intervention or direction of divine providence can obviously never be established by historico-critical means. If it is accepted, it will be on other and antecedent grounds that belong to the sphere of faith.

These antecedent grounds are nowhere discussed by ARCIC: they are assumed. The contention that the primacy of the Bishop of Rome emerged under the guiding providence of the Holy Spirit presupposes a particular view of divine providence that is not uncontroversial. It assumes that God has a plan or design for the Church that incorporates the details of its administrative structure and geographical distribution. It takes for granted that this particular development – and not conflicting developments such as the autonomy of the Orthodox churches or the separation of the Protestant churches – is due to providence. What the Commission is doing (and in this it is following ecclesiastical apologetic old and new) is to bestow a retrospective *imprimatur* on the way things have turned out in history.

I do not believe that we can read the will and purpose of God in this way and I am fairly sure that in their better moments neither do the members – Catholic or Anglican – of the

Commission. The unfortunate members of ARCIC are likely to be told by both sides that they would have done better to have admitted that primacy remains an intractable problem and a barrier to unity, though not necessarily to intercommunion. My own instinct leads me to exercise extreme caution – perhaps verging on scepticism – with regard to appeals to the providence of God. This uneasiness belongs to the spirit of the Enlightenment and is much more pervasive in Anglicanism than in Roman Catholicism. But I recognize that not everyone will be content to leave it there and some will want to go on to make more positive assertions of the providential ordering of the Church.

An example of this in the Anglican tradition is found in Charles Gore's *Roman Catholic Claims*. Gore believed in a providential purpose in the papacy – just as he did in the emergence of the threefold ministry – but one that had become perverted from its divine intention. Contrasting, as it was his characteristic method to do, the papacy of Pius IX with the Church of the fathers, Gore concluded that the papacy represented 'the triumph of imperial absolutism over representative, constitutional authority, and of centralization over consentient witness and co-operation' (pp. 110, 124). Gore was convinced that in the formative centuries of Christianity the papacy had played a providential role, but added that this was comparable to that of the Roman empire and the Greek language.

However, for Gore this recognition of a providential pattern in the history of the Church does not entail the consequences that Roman Catholic claims adduce.

> It does not carry with it any recognition of a dogmatic authority given either to East or West in isolation, nor does it carry with it any implication that the vocation we recognize is part of the church's unalterable system. Any vocation which is rooted in the circumstances of a particular epoch may vanish with the circumstances which conditioned it . . . The very symbol or instrument of unity in one age may be the source of schism in another (p. 109).

Gore's view that in one historical context the papacy may well have had a divine mission, but that mission is not in perpetuity and lapses when history moves on, closely echoes Newman in his ill-fated *Tract 90* (1841), in which he attempted to stretch the Thirty-Nine Articles to accommodate the decrees of the Council of Trent. On the question of the papacy, however, Newman is uncompromising. 'Anglicans maintain,' he asserts, 'that the supremacy of the pope is not directly from revelation, but an event in providence.' He lays down his premiss that 'all things may be undone by the agents and causes by which they are done' and draws the conclusion that 'What revelation gives revelation takes away; what providence gives, providence takes away . . . The papacy began in the exertions and passions of men; and what man can make, man can destroy. Its jurisdiction, while it lasted, was "ordained by God"; when it ceased to be, it ceased to claim our obedience.' It was of course at the Reformation that the papacy 'ceased to be' as far as the Church of England was concerned. The Reformers, Newman concludes, 'who could not destroy a ministry, which the apostles began [i.e. episcopacy], could destroy a dominion which the popes founded' (pp. 77f).

The primacy of the Bishop of Rome, one might conclude, is on the agenda for ecumenical discussions, not because we can trace the hand of providence in its pedigree (no one should have the audacity to claim this with any finality), but simply because the papacy exists; it is a fact of life. The Pope exercises primacy over a large part of the Church, and it is legitimate to ask whether this should be extended, by mutual consent, to a further part. The grounds for approaching this question with extreme circumspection lie in the acknowledged problems of pluralism in the Church today, and have been amply aired earlier in this book.

A sophisticated and plausible variation on the theme of Roman primacy emerging in the providence of God is developed by Jean Tillard in his generally irenical and – in a Catholic context – somewhat radical recent work *The Bishop of Rome*. For Tillard also, the papal primacy is not negotiable. It 'belongs to the mystery of the church in her pilgrimage on earth' and to dispense with it would be to do violence to God's plan (p. 193).

In other words, the Pope's primacy is part of the permanent constitution of the Christian faith, not of its transient historical expression. Translated into the terminology of liberal Protestantism, we could say that papal primacy belongs to the kernel not the husk of the Christian religion: it is of the essence of Christianity.

What foundation can Tillard provide for a claim as uncompromising as this? Like ARCIC he believes that an appeal to immediate dominical institution cannot be sustained, but he does not favour the alternative, espoused by ARCIC, of resort to the way things have turned out in history. For Tillard, the primacy of Rome and therefore of its bishop rests on the decisive and determinative witness through martyrdom made by Peter and Paul in the city, events which belong to the realm of 'salvation history'. It is as though they comprised a continuation of the Acts of the Apostles, though Tillard is not deterred by the fact that the New Testament does not record the deaths of Peter and Paul. This momentous event, as Tillard sees it, helps to create and constitute the apostolicity of the Church and remains through history as the criterion of authentic Christianity. Through some kind of trans-historical metaphysic (so we must suppose) the authority of Peter (seconded by that of Paul) continues to operate through the bishops of Rome who are therefore his (rather than Christ's) vicars in the see. It is as though the apostolic authority of the Church has become located sacramentally in the church of the city of Rome (pp. 97, 86).

As well as legitimating the primacy and authority of the Pope, the apostolic nature of his office also restricts and directs it. The Pope's function is pastoral and prophetic. He presides in love over the Church and watches over its well-being. This role 'expresses itself essentially in the fact of telling out the faith, of guiding the understanding and practice of it, of expressing the spirit of the communion of the churches when faced with some interpretation that would distort it, of speaking in the name of the other bishops not to tell them something that they would not know but to proclaim their common understanding of the gospel of God' (p. 92).

107

This is an attractive picture and differs from ARCIC only in emphasis. It is likely to be influential and to be sympathetically received wherever ecumenical discussions tackle the question of primacy. It deserves our careful consideration. We do not need to rehearse the problems, amplified earlier in this book, regarding the prophetic role of the papacy. We can perhaps take it as sufficiently established that 'the prophetic function embodied in the intervention of the bishop of Rome's word', which for Tillard is the most telling aspect of his charge, remains extremely problematical (p. 178).

There is a serious theological weakness in Tillard's concept, and it is shared by the ARCIC proposals on primacy. Vatican II, together with established Catholic tradition, in appealing to the dominical foundation of the papacy, at least had the merit of appearing to found it upon Christ and the gospel. This, as Vatican II proclaims – here approximating closely to the thought of the Reformers – is the one foundation of the Church: 'The mystery of the holy church is manifest in her very foundation, for the Lord Jesus inaugurated her by preaching the good news' (V2, p. 17). But Tillard frankly confesses (though I wonder whether he recognizes the significance of the admission) that 'the hierarchy of the churches was thus determined in relation not to the story of Jesus, but to the apostolic mission and witness' (p. 74). The theology of the Reformation asserts, on the other hand, that only what can be referred directly to the person of Christ and the Christian gospel can be of the essence of Christianity.

Furthermore, it seems extraordinary to place such emphasis on purely contingent geographical factors. Tillard takes note of the fact that the holy sites of our Lord's life – Bethlehem, Nazareth, the Sea of Galilee, Jerusalem – did not become identified with the visible extension and structure of Christianity. But as in the case of the silence of the New Testament about the deaths of Peter and Paul in Rome, Tillard draws not the obvious conclusion – that it does not matter – but the opposite conclusion – that tradition steps in where the Scriptures remain reticent. For him, the focal centres of Christianity are not Bethlehem, Nazareth and Jerusalem, but 'those points on the map of the world where in the power of the Spirit the gospel of God took root in order to spread out among all the peoples of the world' (p. 75). In complete contrast, we find Luther observing that Christ abolished all restrictions of place when he taught that the kingdom of God comes not with observation. It is true, he continued, that without place and body there can be no Church, but these cannot be constitutive of the Church and do not belong to its essential existence. All such matters are free and indifferent (1883, VII, p. 719f).

Supposing all the apostles were martyred at Rome; or all were martyred at Jerusalem; suppose their place of death and burial were unknown; suppose it were known that Judas Iscariot, Barabbas and Simon Magus - that unholy trinity - had died in Rome: could it make any conceivable difference to the Church's freedom to use Rome, Constantinople, Canterbury or Timbuctoo as its elected administrative and pastoral centre on earth? As Karl Barth remarked in reference to the notion of apostolic succession, all these contrivances are an attempt to provide historico-critical proof of the fourth credal attribute - apostolicity - of the Church of our faith (IV, i, p. 714). Tillard's proposals come very close to replacing the doctrine of the indefectibility of the Church catholic with the indefectibility of the local church of the city of Rome. He clearly makes the primacy of the Pope dependent on the primacy of the church in Rome, and the latter in turn dependent on its somehow God-given faithfulness through all the vicissitudes of history to the true apostolic witness of Peter and Paul: 'an almost fleshly link joins the new people of God to the church of that city where Peter and Paul had their seat' (p. 84). That 'fleshly link' is the weakest link in the argument. It substitutes an historical and empirical concept of indefectibility for the true spiritual and eschatological belief in the indestructibility of the Church as the agent of the gospel. It is mesmerized by the historical pageant of the eternal city, Rome, rather than inspired by the vision of the eschatological 'holy city, new Jerusalem, coming down from God out of heaven, prepared as a bride adorned for her husband' (Rev. 21.2).

The Indestructible Church

One of the occupational hazards of ecumenical discussions is that, as each side bends over backwards to give full credit to the other as a valid and authentic expression of the Christian tradition – to show that it accepts the other as a sister in Christ – a premium is put on mutual criticism and a picture of the Church emerges at the end that presents her in a far rosier light than is justified by the reality. Perhaps these are factors that have contributed to the 'ideal' picture of the Church conveyed by ARCIC 1. She dwells at unity with herself, achieves a common mind on any controversial issues that arise, is able to speak to herself and to the world with a single voice through her universal primate, exercising a pastoral and prophetic role. She holds faithfully to 'the truth as it is in Jesus' and cannot fail to reach her God-appointed goal.

Compared with the Church as we know her, ARCIC's description can justifiably be accused of unverifiable assumptions, grandiose claims and a somewhat triumphalist mentality. It seems to have forgotten that the Church's perfection is eschatological. As Luther says, to all appearances the Church is like her bridegroom Christ – 'hacked to pieces, marked with scratches, despised, crucified, mocked' – while in the sight of God she is a pure, holy, spotless dove (1955-, LIV, p. 262). The face of the Church is the face of one who is a sinner: troubled, forsaken, dying and full of distress. She can never be without suffering, persecution and dying – 'yes, not without sin either' (1883-, 7, p. 684).

The Church's indefectibility must be affirmed on the basis not of her inherent virtues but of the faithfulness of God. 'The Lord will not fail his people: neither will he forsake his inheritance' (Ps. 94.14, BCP). Inerrancy and infallibility must not be allowed to intrude on the doctrine of the indefectibility of the Church: they are not eschatological concepts but purportedly empirical ones, attributed to the Church in her pilgrimage.

The history of the Jewish people, read in the light of Romans 9—11 (especially 11.29: 'the gifts and calling of God are

110

irrevocable'), suggests a sounder biblical understanding of indefectibility – a deeply sombre one that includes and survives apostasy, idolatry, the collapse of community structures, radical pluralism, chronic dilution of the faith, dispersion of the faithful, and genocide. The true Church of Jesus Christ is not the multinational corporation of ARCIC 1 or even the ship of state of Vatican II, voyaging serenely onwards on the ocean of truth. She is not susceptible of a fully integrated and unified organizational structure. She exists where 'two or three are gathered together' in the name of Jesus Christ, celebrating the unity that is already their possession through the breaking of the bread and sharing of the cup that the Lord handed on to simple fishermen.

The present task of ecumenical theology is to create the conditions in which the tacit unity of Christians can be realized in and through the inevitable power structures of the visible Church on earth. The dominical question that gives intensity to these efforts is seldom asked when the indefectibility of the Church is being discussed: 'When the Son of Man comes, shall he find faith on the earth?' (Luke 18.8).

7

Unity and Integrity

In both the Roman Catholic and the Anglican Churches, radical pluralism does not yet have an acceptable face. Traditionalist Catholics tend to feel that to admit the principle of legitimate pluralism would be to open the floodgates of doctrinal relativism; and this would be to sell their birthright. Under the present papacy, the dogmatic principle has been reasserted, the brakes have been put on liberal reforms and uniformity has been strengthened at the expense of diversity.

Anglicans, for their part, have been made to realize – notably by Stephen Sykes's *The Integrity of Anglicanism* – that their comfortable comprehensiveness needs theological justification, if it is not to lay itself open to the charge of providing a refuge for woolly thinking, intellectual dishonesty and ecclesiological hypocrisy. Postponing for a moment any attempt to meet this very necessary challenge, it seems to me that a theological validation of the principle of pluralism might be in order. A positive approach might be indicated along the following lines.

Positive Pluralism

A basic axiom of Christian theism provides the seed-bed for theological pluralism. The doctrine of the transcendence of God implies that no one set of theological statements can adequately describe him. He transcends every attempt to grasp his nature. There thus arises the possibility of a plurality of approaches to the divine mystery. Such approaches may in practice be hard to reconcile or they may appear to be mutually contradictory – this would call for rigorous theological analysis and research and they would have to be argued on their merits – but they should not be ruled out *a priori* simply on the grounds that they speak a different language or approach the object of theological enquiry from a fresh angle. Pluralism in the Church may be a legitimate response to the mystery of God.

Furthermore, the bare notion of unity in diversity needs no further initial justification than to point to the presence of this principle in the trinitarian nature of God – whether conceived of in its highest objective form, three persons sharing one nature, or in its lowest subjective form, three modes in which one divine presence and action are experienced. So the principle of unity in diversity finds its incontestable mandate at the most axiomatic level of Christian discourse.

Recent biblical scholarship has exposed a plurality of theologies within the Bible itself, in both the Old Testament and the New. As C.F. Evans has remarked of the New Testament, in *Christian Believing*, its various contributory theologies simply may have to lie side by side, unreconciled, since they may be – and may have been intended to be – irreconcilable in some respects (pp. 43–51). Paul and James on faith and works is a case in point: as basic data of theological construction, it is possible to reconcile them in an ultimate synthesis, but as they stand it is not easy to make them agree except by sleight of hand. James Dunn, drawing attention to the diverse *kerygmata* of apostolic preaching and pointing out that one underlying *kerygma* can only be discovered in the New Testament by a process of abstraction, has concluded that, 'If the New Testament is any guide, one can never say: This particular formulation is the gospel for all time and for every situation' (pp. 30ff). The principle of pluralism is thus ineradicably imprinted on the foundation documents of Christianity.

The same richness of pluralism enables the Church to transcend cultural barriers and protects her from sinking into a culturally insular orthodoxy under the illusion that it is timeless universal truth. Here the principle of unity in diversity reflects a central attribute of the Christian gospel, its universality as a message that is to be preached to 'every creature' and to bring to God 'a great multitude that no man could number of all nations and kindreds and people and tongues' (Mark 16.15; Rev. 7.9). At least one of the several

113

facets of the Church's pluriform message may appeal to individuals of diverse social, cultural and educational backgrounds. Pastoral experience bears out the observation that not a few who lose their faith in times of crisis might have been helped by a fuller acquaintance with the riches of the Christian tradition: their own traditions were too narrow or superficial to offer the needed help, but it does not follow that Christianity itself had failed.

Radical developments in Roman Catholic theology from Newman to Vatican II and the work of Rahner and Lonergan reflect this concern. Newman gave, as one cause of the development of doctrine, the challenge of meeting a new cultural context: 'If Christianity be a universal religion, suited not to one locality or period, but to all times and places, it cannot but vary in its relations and dealings towards the world around it, that is, it will develop.' Principles must be adapted to persons and circumstances; they 'must be thrown into new shapes' determined by the society in which they are to operate (1974, p. 150). Rahner echoes this when he remarks that God's revelation is 'directed through the medium of the historical process at the total history of humanity' (I, p. 47). Lonergan's conviction that his cognitional theory is common to every diverse human culture and that his method can 'home in' on the truth of faith in every cultural disguise, enables him to take a very relaxed approach to the question of adapting the Christian gospel to different cultures. Lonergan insists that to preach the gospel to all nations is 'to preach it to every class in every culture in the manner that accords with the assimilative powers of that class and culture'. This preaching will have to be 'as multiform as are the diverse brands of common sense generated by the many languages, social forms, and cultural meanings and values of mankind' (1972, p. 328). He warns that we need to discriminate between the gospel itself on the one hand, and the gospel in the form into which it has evolved within our own culture, on the other. In preaching the gospel as it has been developed within our own culture, we are preaching not only the gospel but our own culture, and therefore asking others not only to accept the gospel but also to renounce their own culture and to accept ours. Classicist uniformity of culture was never more than 'the shabby shell of Catholicism' (1972, pp. 262f, 327). The 'functional specialities' of Lonergan's method, especially that of 'communications', are intended to facilitate those adaptations of the gospel that make it culturally relevant, without sacrificing its permanent truth-claims. Regarded in this light, pluralism in the Church can become an aspect of catholicity.

If Christianity is not primarily an ideology (a system of culture-specific meanings) to be preserved, defended, and propagated, but is rather a venture of faith and life, an exploration into truth and reality, it must always remain open to new and unsuspected factors that may emerge, pointing the way to fresh lines of enquiry or providing the tools for self-criticism and reconstruction. A.N. Whitehead has drawn attention to the enormous potential to be found in ideas that sleep in forgotten systems of thought. Pluralism in the Church encourages the cross-fertilization of ideas that may lead to new departures (1942, p. 173).

Pluralism within a given church merely mirrors the pluralism of Christianity as a world-religion: it is a microcosm of the world Church. Ecclesiological work in the internal forum can constitute a pilot study for the whole ecumenical enterprise in the external forum. It was in this sense that the report *Catholicity* claimed that Anglican comprehensiveness opens the way for the Church of England to become 'a school of synthesis' for the benefit of the Church catholic. If the Roman Catholic Church can also work out an acceptable rationale for its own irreversible diversity, it will perform a service for the whole Church and enhance the prospects for meaningful moves towards unity.

Finally, it is surely indispensable for every ecclesiology that it should be marked by a certain realism about the prospects for putting it into practice. In his *Prophetical Office of the Church* (1838), Newman remarked that while 'Protestantism and Popery' were 'real religions', the *via media*, recovered by the Tractarians from the seventeeth-century English divines, had scarcely existed 'except on paper'. The Tractarian experiment

115

was an attempt to implement it, not merely in isolated parishes like Newman's Littlemore or Keble's Hursley, but on the scale of a national church (pp. 20f). In his later period of disillusionment, Newman was compelled to admit failure – the *via media* had never got beyond a paper theory.

We have already had occasion to complain that the ARCIC documents 'romanticize' about the Church – specifically, about the possibilities of consensus, the realities of power structures and ecclesiastical bureaucracy, and the Church's possession of the truth. This criticism is also made by Stephen Sykes in a telling critique, 'ARCIC and the Papacy', where he questions the propriety of asking Anglicans to approve an 'ideal' papacy when by doing so they may be letting themselves in for the papacy as it actually is (p. 14f). Rome has not yet implemented the consultative procedures envisaged by Vatican II. Its recognition of pluralism has been muted and half-hearted. Recent disciplinary episodes reveal that there is at present no intention of embracing the implications of the modern pluralistic situation in a liberal culture. To this extent, the official Roman Catholic attitude can be accused of cultivating an ostrich-like air of unreality.

On the other hand, the acceptance of pluralism as we find it in the Anglican Church denotes the eminent realism of Anglicanism. There is no need to apologize too much for the alleged defects of Anglicanism – its lack of discipline, its reticence where dogmatic definitions are concerned, its breadth of permitted opinion. Its pragmatism is not always born of a weary cynicism: at its best it is the product of sagacity, a sense of realism about the world as it is in the providence of God, a willingness to look the facts in the face and to make the best of them. In other words, Anglicanism is not seduced by Utopian and perfectionist ecclesiologies. It takes seriously the fallenness of the world, the brokenness of the Church and the frailty of human nature.

Concepts of Comprehensiveness

Yet one of the obstacles to unity between the Roman Catholic and the Anglican Churches - one that is not always visible on the surface of ecumenical dialogue but lurks beneath like a great submerged rock on which the ship of unity seems doomed to founder - is Roman Catholic perplexity, sometimes amounting to suspicion, about the permitted latitude of belief in Anglicanism.

Rahner has pointed out that theological freedom has been allowed to go so far in the Protestant churches generally that reunion with Rome is not feasible (XVI, p. 247). In its *Observations*, the Sacred Congregation for the Doctrine of the Faith expressed surprise that the ARCIC *Final Report* did not provide documentation from the Anglican formularies to the extent that it did from Roman Catholic sources. In a further response, Cardinal Ratzinger asks for Anglicans to be more forthcoming about where precisely authority lies in their tradition.

The Anglican members of ARCIC have been compelled to play the game by Catholic rules. Without explicitly appealing to the Anglican formularies (in some cases this would have been difficult!), they have been made to come down off the fence. Stephen Sykes has astutely asked, in 'ARCIC and the Papacy', whether this implies a 'reconfessionalization' of Anglicanism, with all the implications that this would have for its much vaunted comprehensiveness, or whether Roman Catholic ecclesiology is being stretched to embrace a plurality of views - a spread of approved options.

It is now imperative - not only for reasons of Anglican integrity, but also as a contribution to ecumenism - to establish an acceptable rationale for Anglican comprehensiveness, since it is inconceivable that Anglicanism's liberal terms of communion, its comprehensiveness or pluralism, could ever be abandoned in favour of a reconfessionalization of the church. These battles have been fought before.

Comprehensiveness was once 'the glory of the Church of England'. The authors of *Catholicity* (1947) claimed that it opened the way for the Church of England to become 'a school of synthesis over a wider field than any other church in Christendom' (p. 49). But not even the most fervent Anglican apologist would claim that this potentiality has even begun to be realized. Far from being able to give a lead to other traditions, the Church of England has done little to explore the possibilities for synthesis within its own communion. The whole notion of comprehensiveness has recently been pilloried from within the Anglican fold by Stephen Sykes as intellectually bankrupt and morally suspect.

If comprehensiveness is to be rehabilitated within Anglicanism itself and the principle of unity in diversity defended as an acceptable and even essential characteristic of a united Church of the future, a constructive and positive interpretation of this concept needs to be offered. Perhaps I have already said enough to make out a *prima facie* case for pluralism – to show that it need not be merely a let-out for lazy minds trying to prop up corrupt churches. But the need to develop a theological justification for this much abused and much exploited notion remains. The question is whether there is an understanding of pluralism in the Church open to us that does not seem to imply 'a plurality of Lords, a plurality of spirits and a plurality of gods', to borrow Barth's phrase (IV. i, p. 675).

In what follows, I suggest three ways in which the notion of comprehensiveness has been employed, all inadequate, before I go on in the next section, to outline an interpretation that I am prepared to defend. Though I illustrate my argument primarily from Anglicanism, the case I am trying to make will have immediate relevance to our vision of a united church in which Anglican and Roman Catholic traditions will be incorporated. The first way is that of mere juxtaposition of views – the interpretation of comprehensiveness raised by many writers on Anglicanism and disowned with contempt – while confessing that this is how Anglican claims of comprehensiveness strike the observer from without (and even from within!)

Forty years ago, Hensley Henson commented that the Church of England exhibited a doctrinal incoherence un-paralleled in the orthodox Christian tradition (p. 108). Compare this with the contemporary assessment of E.L. Mascall, 'reached with reluctance and distress and after long and anxious thought, that the theological activity of the Anglican churches is in a condition of extreme, though strangely complacent, confusion, and that this is having a disastrously demoralizing effect upon the life and thought of the church as a whole and of the pastoral clergy in particular' (p. 1). Charles Gore asserted that comprehensiveness envisaged as the mere juxtaposition of views gave us not a Church but 'a mere consensus of jarring atoms' (1914, pp. 4f). Alec Vidler similarly rejects as 'unprincipled syncretism' the sort of comprehensiveness that has been taken to mean (by whom, he does not say) that 'it is the glory of the Church of England to hold together in juxtaposition as many varieties of Christian faith and practice as are willing to agree to differ, so that the church is regarded as a sort of league of religions' (p. 165). The Archbishop's report *Catholicity* (1947), observing that the possibilities of synthesis within Anglicanism remain largely unrealized, concludes with studied understatement that 'it is by no means true' that the mere juxtaposition of diverse elements in Anglicanism will produce this synthesis (p. 51).

This view of comprehensiveness as opposing elements lying side by side has probably never received attempted theological justification, but that does not prevent its being tacitly accepted by a wide section of theologically apathetic clergy and ecclesiologically bewildered laity. Those who are overtly party-minded render support to this view by adhering to the party that in their view enjoys a virtual monopoly of truth, while continuing as a members of a church which tolerates opposed, and therefore (in their view) erroneous opinions.

A second view of comprehensiveness is based on compromise. This is what the celebrated Anglican *via media* often amounts to - a halfway house, an Aristotelian golden mean, the pedestrian pursuit of a safe middle path through all extremes. This view goes back to the seventeenth century, when George Herbert compared the charms of the Church of England - 'A fine aspect in fit array, Neither too mean nor yet too gay' - with the allurements of Rome, the painted harlot on the hill, and the uncomeliness of the Protestant churches, the slovenly wench in the valley, declaring, 'But dearest Mother, (what those miss) The *mean* thy praise and glory is.' Simon Patrick praised 'that virtuous mediocrity which our church observes between the meretricious gaudiness of the Church of Rome and the squalid sluttery of fanatic conventicles'.

The Preface (1662) to the Book of Common Prayer seems to echo these sentiments when it asserts: 'It hath been the wisdom of the Church of England, ever since the first compiling of her Publick Liturgy, to keep the mean between the two extremes, of too much stiffness in refusing, and of too much easiness in admitting any variation from it.' For George Savile, Marquess of Halifax, the Church of England was 'a Trimmer between the frenzy of fanatic visions and the lethargic ignorance of popish dreams'.

The Whig historian Macaulay gave this interpretation of Anglicanism his imprimatur. Her constitution, doctrines and services bear the marks of the compromise from which the Church of England was born. She occupies a middle position between the churches of Rome and Geneva. While her doctrinal standards would have met with the approval of Calvin or Knox, her prayers, derived from the ancient breviaries, 'are such that Cardinal Fisher or Cardinal Pole might have heartily joined in them.' Similarly with the ministry: while Rome maintained the doctrine of apostolic succession and many Protestants rejected episcopacy altogether, the Anglican Reformers took a middle course. They retain bishops without making episcopacy of the *esse* of the Church or necessary to guarantee the efficacy of her sacraments. Though rejecting the doctrine of transubstantiation and all forms of sacramental adoration she nevertheless, 'to the disgust of the Puritan, required her children to receive the memorials of divine love, meekly kneeling upon their knees.' 'Though sacramental confession was no longer obligatory, she gently invited the dying penitent to confess his sins to a divine, and empowered her ministers to soothe the departing soul by an absolution, which breathes the very spirit of the old religion' (I, p. 47). William Temple, whose facility for devising reconciling formulae is well known, seems to sponsor this view of comprehensiveness. An exclusive loyalty to either the Reformation or the unreformed Catholic tradition is not a viable option for Anglicans, he claims. 'The Church of England has always bridged the gulf (or sat on the hedge, if you like) that divides "catholic" and "protestant" from one another' (1958, p. 88).

This understanding of comprehensiveness as compromise does attempt to do justice to one deep-seated and permanent element in Anglicanism – its moderation, its stress on sobriety, balance and the horror of 'enthusiasm'; what Newman in *The Prophetical Office* called its 'characteristic calmness and caution' (p. 26). A critic might call it Anglicanism's Laodicean lukewarmness, its propensity to muddle through, its dislike of pushing principles to their logical conclusions – what Hensley Henson called 'its almost limitless acquiescence in anomalies which are practically convenient, its ready condonation of admitted abuses which serve material interests' (p. 65). This apparently ineradicable element acts as a useful check on hasty innovation and creates an ethos uncongenial to movements centred on charismatic individuals, but its drawbacks are precisely superficiality, complacency and lack of vision. As the authors of *Catholicity* justly remark, to interpret comprehensiveness as compromise seems to presuppose that grey possesses the virtues of both black and white: the result is 'an insipid centrality which misses the truth of catholic and evangelical alike and is no more comprehensive than either of them' (p. 51). The real trouble with this view of the *via media*, remarks E.A. de Mendietta, a Roman Catholic convert to Anglicanism, is its 'chronic tendency towards complacency and mediocrity'. The so-called central or moderate position reflects neither the breadth nor the depth of the Anglican synthesis, of 'its meeting and merging of all the living values of catholicism and evangelicalism' (pp. 49f). It often takes someone coming to Anglicanism from outside, as de Mendietta did, to tell us what it is all about.

According to a third approach, Anglican comprehensiveness is eclectic; it gives the freedom to pick and choose from the available theological options. 'I condemn not all things in the Councell of Trent nor approve all in the Synod of Dort,' declares Sir Thomas Browne in the *Religio Medici* (p. 8). Anglicanism, claimed Gore, represents a combination which has the potential to renew Catholicism world wide. The glory of the Anglican Church, according to Gore, is that at the Reformation she retained the traditional structure of Catholicism - creeds, canon, hierarchy, sacraments - while opening her arms to the new learning of the Renaissance: the new appeal to Scripture, the freedom of historical criticism and the duty of private judgement (1892, p. 36). Put like this, it seems as though Anglicanism wants to have its cake and eat it. As R.W. Church pointed out, writing at the same time as Gore, this ideal seems to many to be 'an illogical and incomprehensible attempt to unite incompatible principles and elements.' It leaves the contributory elements lying side by side: it does not explain how they are to be combined (1896, p. 69).

Towards a Synthesis

When F.D. Maurice speaks of a union of positive principles and Michael Ramsey of a binding together of the gospel, the Catholic Church and sound learning, they are not envisaging a mere juxtaposition of elements, a compromise between competing claims or a fastidious selection of what appeals from among a broad range of theological options. Nor are they advocating a view of comprehensiveness on the lines of complementarity - commonly understood in a way that approximates to the medieval idea of the 'double truth'. When they advocate 'an embracing of the positive truths of our tradition in their depth and vigour,' they are speaking (in the case of Maurice, explicitly; in the case of Michael Ramsey, probably implicitly) from within a distinct and powerful epistemology which alone makes such a combination possible. It does this according to the mode of polarity, operating in the tacit dimension. Let me explain.

The doctrine of polarity has remote and recondite origins, shading off into mythology and the occult. But it is not this esoteric sense of polarity that is meant when, for example, H.R. McAdoo, the Anglican Co-Chairman of ARCIC I, asserts that polarity or a 'quality of living tension' is an overall characteristic of Anglican theological method. It is in the weaker sense of truths-in-tension that polarity distinguishes the Anglican theology of the seventeenth century.

'Beneath the surface,' writes McAdoo, 'was the feeling for the *via media* which was not in its essence compromise or an intellectual expedient but a quality of thinking, an approach in which elements usually regarded as mutually exclusive were seen to be in fact complementary. These things were held in a living tension, not in order to walk the tight-rope of compromise, but because they were seen to be mutually illuminating and to fertilize each other.' This synthesis incorporated the authority of Scripture and the freedom of reason, credal orthodoxy and liberty in non-essentials, the appeal to antiquity and the welcome to new knowledge, the historic continuity of the Church and the freedom of national churches (pp. 312f).

In the early nineteenth century, however, under the influence of German idealist metaphysics, the notion of polarity became more explicitly defined. In our present context, it owes its formulation to Coleridge and is integral to the Platonic stream of philosophical theology that regards him as its presiding spirit, F.D. Maurice being its most powerful exponent. In his study of Coleridge and Bentham, John Stuart Mill commented that no one's synthesis can be more complete than his analysis (p. 58). Coleridge pointed out that analysis may *divide* or it may *distinguish*. The difference is crucial to Coleridge, for to divide is often to destroy, while to distinguish is often to discern a polarity. 'It is a dull and obtuse mind,' Coleridge remarks in *Aids to Reflection*, 'that must divide in order to distinguish'. To divide is the work of a *keen* mind; to distinguish without dividing (i.e. in polarity), the achievement of a *subtle* mind. Turning from analysis to synthesis: the function of polarity here derives from Coleridge's belief that men are usually right in what they positively affirm but wrong in what they negate. In the old saying, 'Extremes meet', Coleridge found the key to reducing apparent contradictions to complementary truths held in tension.

F.D. Maurice's doctrine of the union of opposites owed its intensity to the circumstances of his upbringing in a household torn by sectarian strife, and its paradoxical twist to Coleridge's teaching on polarity. Maurice's passionate search for unity in diversity is symbolized by his transition from unitarianism to trinitarian orthodoxy - here too he was following Coleridge. He rejected the idea that the Anglicanism that emerged from the Elizabethan settlement of religion was a cowardly or cunning compromise which lacked the courage to ally itself either with the radical Reformers like John Knox or with 'the bold reactionaries of the Council of Trent.' He believed that the secret of Elizabeth I's success rested on her unique ability to unite in herself the reformed and catholic elements in the nation. 'The alkali and the acid produced a healthy effervescence; no neutral salt had as yet resulted from their combination' (1872, II, pp. 138ff).

Maurice had an equal horror of both systems and electicism. The Catholic Church was constituted by the union of positive living principles which, isolated by sectarian systems, had there lost their life and power. While the systems continued to witness to these principles, they at the same time tended to distort them. Maurice did not hold that the systems as such could be reconciled, only that the positive, living principles to which each bore witness could form parts of a higher truth. 'There is a divine harmony, of which the living principle in each of these systems forms one note, of which the systems themselves are a disturbance and a violation' (1958, II, p. 322).

The constructive approach to opposing systems is not by capitulating to one or the other but, by sympathetic insight, bringing to light the deepest aspirations of those who are ensnared by them. Maurice is echoing Coleridge when he claims that the positive aspects of opposing views are 'always struggling towards each other and are kept apart only by the negative and contradictory elements with which they are mingled.' For example, the Tractarians were right to want to 'catholicize' the Church of England but wrong when they vowed to 'unprotestantize' it. Maurice does not mean by this that the Church is to be half Protestant and half Catholic, but rather that she is to be 'most Catholic when she is most Protestant' (1843, pp. 20, 12).

The principle of unity in diversity is firmly anchored in the very structure of Christian theism and a degree of pluralism is now a permanent feature, not only of the Anglican Church, but of all Christian churches. But the ecclesiological integrity of the churches hangs upon the way in which they understand and respond to this problem. We cannot with integrity accept comprehensiveness as mere juxtaposition, or as compromise, or as eclecticism: a deeper synthesis than these is required and the notion of polarity may indicate the mode in which that synthesis can be achieved.

I am not arguing for an esoteric, mythological, occult notion of polarity, nor am I claiming that it needs to be understood in terms of Hegelian dialectic. This is not the place to attempt a philosophical discussion of the notion of polarity or to bring out its importance in theological method. The concept commends itself to the Christian mind as soon as we reflect on the pattern into which Christian experience seems naturally to fall – a pattern shaped by the polarities of revelation and reason, transcendence and immanence, grace and nature. These form the basic conceptual configuration of theology and transcend confessional differences. They constitute the grammar of faith.

Dialogue between the churches, in the present radically pluralistic situation, raises the question of what they have in common in the final analysis. The search for common ground is usually confined to fundamental tenets of doctrine. But might it not be the case that there is also a tacit grammar of faith, subsisting below the threshold of explicit theology, which is capable of being brought out into the open and shown to be a significant dimension of the essential unity of churches? This links up with Karl Rahner's call for ecumenical theology to take more seriously the inchoate, inarticulate faith of lay Christians which seems so serenely to bypass the dialectics and polemics of official theology (XIV, pp. 248ff, 266f). It is in this realm of the tacit sense of a shared faith that a practical basis for Christian unity is going to be discovered.

Unity in the Personal Dimension

Creative exponents of Anglican theological method (Coleridge in *Aids to Reflection*, Maurice in *The Kingdom of Christ* and Michael Ramsey in *The Gospel and the Catholic Church*) challenge the churches to engage in a dialogue that operates in the mode of personal knowledge, not at the level of mutual accommodation, trading of concessions and bargaining counters – cut-price transactions that do not carry conviction because they are not true to the traditions represented. They call upon us to learn the art of distinguishing without dividing – at the level of faith and praxis, not of dogmatic propositions – between Protestant and Catholic, individual and corporate, spontaneous and formal, immanent and transcendent elements in the wholeness of Christian experience. They invite us to allow ourselves to be guided by the positive affirmations that different traditions have to offer, rather than being diverted by their polemical denials. They teach us to train ourselves to look beneath the surface for the spiritual aspirations and insights that may be veiled by historical or cultural forms.

But it is necessary to stress that when Coleridge speaks of distinguishing without dividing, Maurice of the craving of the spirit for truth and the tendency of positive truths to coalesce, and Michael Ramsey of a binding together in synthesis of disparate elements in ecclesiology, they are presupposing a particular philosophy of mind. They are assuming the reality of a tacit dimension – the creative, constructive and heuristic power of thinking below the threshold of explicit consciousness.

The notion of truths-in-tension, of polarity, needs to be considered in the light of a particular epistemological tradition, stemming from the Platonists of antiquity and passing, through German idealism and the thought of Coleridge, into modern thought, where it has received reinforcement and restatement from philosophers of mind such as Whitehead, Polanyi, Popper and Lonergan. Polarity cannot be grafted on to a merely analytical and discursive mode of rationality. It flourishes in a context provided by our grasp of the power of intuition, the reality of tacit knowledge and the transcendent operations of insight whereby we may indeed have a real though inarticulate sense of the full orbit of Christian truth.

But this is of course no monopoly of theologians, who in this respect stand alongside all their fellow Christians. It will readily be agreed that the faith of most Christian people today - no less than in earlier ages of semi-literacy - is instinctive, intuitive, unthought-out and unarticulated. It is sustained by richness of imagery and association, by a sense of mystery and unexplored depths conveyed by the gospel story, the liturgy and Christian hymnody.

The modern churches are for ever trying to force their members into a supposedly 'higher' state of rationalized belief and self-conscious practice, by stripping the liturgies of their aura of sacred association and substituting two-dimensional, sloganized phraseology that starves the spirit. In this the churches are, I believe, working against their own best interests. No doubt it is good to know what we are saying, to understand what we are reading and, up to a point, to clarify and analyse our beliefs. But on the other hand, we need to ask whether most Christians will ever do this. Pastoral experience suggests that the new liturgies do not make things very much clearer to most churchgoers. They do not use liturgy in that way. They comprehend what they cannot always be said to understand. Furthermore, we need to raise the question of whether what is completely transparent and explicit is worth saying or hearing, bearing in mind that in the liturgy and the Scriptures we enter upon holy ground, we approach a mystery. The music of words and rhythms, the richness of symbol and metaphor, the echoes of association and the intimations of what is 'beyond our ken' are the vehicles of shared values and meanings. In this tacit and indirect way (to quote de Burgh) the dim background of human consciousness is brought into contact with the dim background of reality (p. 77).

What we have established about the tacit nature of all significant knowledge and of the faith of Christians in particular, must now be brought to bear on the tasks and prospects of ecumenical theology.

As Karl Rahner has suggested, the vast majority of the members of the Christian churches are members of one such church for historical, geographical, sociological or psychological reasons - not on theological or confessional grounds.

Most may be quite unable to say what makes them Roman Catholics rather than Anglicans, or Lutherans rather than Reformed. Their faith is not concerned with such questions. They recognize that their fellow Christians of other traditions share the same hope, participate in the same salvation and follow the same Lord. Although unable to reconcile confessional differences of creed or practice, we enjoy an unquestioned unity at the tacit level. The same Spirit cries out without words to the same Father in our hearts (Rom. 8.15). 'In the Spirit of God all of us "know" something more simple, more true and more real than we can know or express at the level of our theological concepts' (XIV, pp. 248ff, 266f; XVII, pp. 199f). As Lonergan reminds us, the true basis of unity is the fact that God's love has been shed abroad in our hearts by the Holy Spirit (Rom. 5.5) (1972, p. 327).

It is this implicit or tacit faith – 'the faith that is lived, which counts before God and brings salvation', rather than the official, stated faith of the churches – that forms the starting point of ecumenical theology. We are in touch with reality at the level of faith and praxis. Theological propositions are secondary and derivative: they can only reflect the divine reality that we encounter in Christian experience, at several removes. Such propositions do not produce progress in the truth, so why should the quest for unity be spearheaded by theologians sitting round a table comparing propositions? That is to put the cart before the horse.

As Rahner has pointed out, this tacit unity that already exists among Christians – though it provides the initial impetus for ecumenism – has not been allowed to influence the course taken by ecumenical efforts. But progress in the cause of unity will only come when the leaders of the churches cease to treat their lay members like children who need to be chaperoned, and set them free to explore in their own time and way the unity that, already their possession, waits to be fully entered into.

The clear logic of the position is this: the living Christ through his Spirit in the world has created a fellowship of those who, believing in the same gospel and sharing the same baptism, find a grace of unity in their common salvation. Their great desire is to share together in the sacrament of unity, the Eucharist, and to obey their Lord's command, 'Do this in remembrance of me.'

As has been sufficiently implied in this book, it is unrealistic to hope that an adequate measure of doctrinal accord can be attained between the Roman Catholic Church as she now is, with her dogmatic principle still virtually intact, and the Anglican Church with its incorrigible pluralism, for a plenary, structured union to take place in the foreseeable future. While the long-term strategy of theological agreement continues to be worked at, the immediate goal should be to establish what the minimum requirements for intercommunion would be.

Radical Ecumenical Theology

In conclusion we must ask what the criteria are of a radical ecumenical theology. What makes a theology both radical and ecumenical? In contemporary usage the word 'radical' means either critical and subversive or penetrating and fundamental. A theology of the Church and of its stewardship of Christian truth, along the lines sketched in the preceding chapters, will aim to be radical in both senses.

First, it will be *critical*. As we have seen, both Karl Rahner from the Roman Catholic side and William Temple from the Anglican side called, in their different ways, for an attitude of acutely intelligent criticism, appreciation and evaluation of the Christian tradition, bringing to bear all the resources, all the insights, of sacred and secular learning. As Nicholas Lash has claimed, theology is 'irreducibly interrogative in character'.

By the same token, a radical ecumenical theology will be *subversive*. Theology that is doing its job will be subversive of forms of belief and practice that can be shown to be ecclesiastical expressions of obscurantism, self-interest, prejudice, exploitation or oppression. It will disturb stereotyped assumptions about what the Bible teaches and what earlier Christians have believed. It will be subversive of the patronizing attitude to the past and the complacent attitude to the present that go hand in hand. As Nicholas Lash has recently

129

remarked (in the *Times*), 'If theologians do their work well, they will upset people not because they set out to shock them, but because good theology . . . subverts our common preference for a quiet life and our desire to have our prejudices confirmed as fact.'

Second, such a theology will be *penetrating*. In the literal sense of radical, an adequate ecclesiology will penetrate to the root of the matter. Enlisting the help of the sociology of religion, it will aim to probe to the deepest source of our divisions. It will not be content to compare doctrines as they stand, taking them at their face value, but will ask what needs they originally fulfilled, what insistent requirements of praxis, in liturgy, pastoral ministry, ecclesiastical discipline, social cohesion, etc. they embodied, and whether these are still valid.

Then it will be *foundational*. A radical ecumenical theology will attempt to uncover once again the fundamental nature of the Christian Church, 'the Church's one foundation'. In this it will be guided by St Paul's admonition: 'Other foundation can no man lay, than that which is laid which is Jesus Christ' (1 Cor. 3.11). It will be impressed by the intensity of the Reformers' quest for the Christological centre of the Church's existence, which had the effect of relegating to the periphery aspects of ecclesiology that could not be directly grounded upon this centre. It will be encouraged by the Second Vatican Council's determination to find the origins of the Church in the gospel preached by the Lord Jesus Christ (V2, pp. 17, 39).

So a radical ecumenical theology will certainly not be radical in the popular sense of being mesmerized by the latest theological trends or social theories, blown about by every wind of doctrine, uncommitted to the life of the Church as she exists now, scornful of what we have inherited, destructively critical of what we have been given.

Theology is 'irreducibly interrogative in character' in the sense that it puts its questions to that massive deposit of Christian faith and life, the vast substance of what is given, the tradition from which we draw our spiritual life and nurture. Within that great polymorphous tradition each one of us has a home, Anglican, Roman, Orthodox, Lutheran, Reformed or whatever it may be. On our own part of the mountain of faith we quarry away, mining rich ore to enrich the Church or fuel its mission. We see the great mountain from our own vantage point, though we try to get an idea of the whole. But inevitably our theology - ecumenical as it should and must be - will bear the stamp of its origins. It will be a Roman Catholic ecumenical theology or a Lutheran ecumenical theology. The chapters of this book attempt the groundwork - and it is merely groundwork, an agenda, combining principles and polemics - of an Anglican ecumenical theology.

There is a difference between a confessional theology, on the one hand, and an ecumenical theology written from within a confessional tradition, on the other. This book owes as much to Luther as it does to Hooker; it draws heavily on Newman, who spans Anglican and Roman theology; the most frequently cited author is probably Rahner. For as we quarry away on the mountain of the faith, it sometimes happens that suddenly the face crumbles, light pours in and we break through into tunnels where others are working a rich vein. We are freely offered a share of their treasure.

BIBLIOGRAPHY

Place of publication is London unless stated.

⋆Abbott, E.S. et al., eds., 1952, *Catholicity, A Study in the Conflict of Christian Traditions in the West* (Report to the Archbishop of Canterbury 1947).

Abbott, W.M., ed., 1966, *The Documents of Vatican II* (abbrev. V2).

Adam, K., 1938, *The Spirit of Catholicism.*

Anglican Consultative Council, see Sykes.

Anglican-Orthodox Dialogue: The Dublin Agreed Statement; 1985.

Anglican-Roman Catholic International Commission, 1982, *The Final Report* (abbrev. ARCIC, cited by page and paragraph).

Augustine, 1972, *The City of God.* Penguin.

Avis, P.D.L., 1976, 'Polarity and Reductionism' (*Scottish Journal of Theology,* 29, pp. 401-13).

1980, 'Polarity and Pluriformity in the Church' (*King's Theological Review,* 3, pp. 55-64).

1982a, *The Church in the Theology of the Reformers.*

1982b, 'In the Shadow of the Frankfurt School: From "Critical Theory" to "Critical Theology"' (*Scottish Journal of Theology,* 35, pp. 529-40).

1983a, 'Luther's Theology of the Church' (*Churchman,* 97, pp. 104-11).

1983b, 'The Church's Journey into Truth: A Preface to Further Anglican-Roman Catholic Dialogue' (*Theology,* 86, pp. 403-11).

1984, 'Does Natural Theology Exist?' (*Theology,* 87, pp. 431-7).

Gore: Construction and Conflict. Cambridge (forthcoming).

The Methods of Modern Theology (forthcoming).

'The Tractarian Challenge to Consensus and the Identity of Anglicanism' (*King's Theological Review,* forthcoming).

Balthasar, see von Balthasar

Barth, K., 1956-, *Church Dogmatics.* Edinburgh.

Berkouwer, G.C., 1976, *The Church* in *Studies in Dogmatics.* Grand Rapids.

Blanshard, B., 1939, *The Nature of Thought.*

Bradley, F.H., 1914, *Essays on Truth and Reality.* Oxford.

Browne, T. 1909, *Religio Medici.* Oxford.

Bultmann, R., 1964, *Aletheia, Theological Dictionary of the New Testament,* I, ed., G. Kittel; trans., G.W. Bromiley. Grand Rapids.

Burgh, see de Burgh.

Burnet, G., 1845, *An Exposition of the XXXIX Articles of the Church of England* by Gilbert Bishop of Sarum. Oxford.

Bibliography

Butler, J., 1889, *The Analogy of Religion, Natural and Revealed.*

Calvin, J., n.d., *Institutes of the Christian Religion*, tr., H. Beveridge.

Catholic Church, *Doctrinal Documents*, see Neuner.

Catholicity, see Abbott, E.S.

Chadwick, W.O., 1983, *Newman*. Oxford.

Chirico, P., 1977, *Infallibility: The Crossroads of Doctrine.*

Church, R.W., 1891, *The Oxford Movement.*

    1896, *Pascal and Other Sermons.*

Clark and Davey, eds., 1974, *Anglican/Roman Catholic Dialogue: The Work of the Preparatory Commission.*

Cloud of Unknowing, The, 1961. Penguin.

Coleridge, S.T., 1893, *Aids to Reflection.*

    1895, *Anima Poetae.*

    1969, *The Friend* in *Collected Works*, ed., B. Rooke, Princeton.

Congar, Y., 1959, *Lay People in the Church.*

    1970, 'Infaillibilité et Indéfectibilité' (*Revue des Sciences Philosophiques et Théologiques*, 54, pp. 601-18).

    1984, *Diversity and Communion.*

Coulson, J., 1970, *Newman and the Common Tradition.* Oxford.

    1981, *Religion and Imagination: 'in aid of a grammar of assent'.* Oxford.

Davis, C., 1980, *Theology and Political Society.* Cambridge.

de Burgh, W.G., 1949, *The Life of Reason.*

de Mendietta, E.A., 1971, *Anglican Vision.*

Denzinger, H.J.D., 1957, *The Sources of Catholic Dogma.* St Louis.

Dionysius the Areopagite, 1940, *The Divine Names* and *The Mystical Theology*, ed., C.E. Rolt.

Doctrinal Documents of the Catholic Church, see Neuner.

Doctrine Commission of the Church of England, 1938, *Doctrine in the Church of England.*

    1976, *Christian Believing.*

    1981, *Believing in the Church.*

Documents of Vatican II, see Abbott, W.M.

Downing, F.G., 1978, 'A Polemic and Against Polemic' (*Theology*, 81, pp. 331-6).

Dunn, J.D.G., 1977, *Unity and Diversity in the New Testament.*

Ewing, A.C., 1977, *Value and Reality.*

Fairweather, E., see Clark and Davey.

Fallows, W.G., 1964, *Mandell Creighton and the English Church.* Oxford.

Farrer, A., see Goulder.

Field, R., 1847, *Of the Church.* Edinburgh.

Fouyas, M., 1972, *Orthodoxy, Roman Catholicism and Anglicanism.* Oxford.

Bibliography

Fuller, R.H., 1981, 'The Authority of the Scriptures in Anglicanism' (*Lutheran-Episcopal Dialogue*, pp. 87-113). Cincinnati.

Gill, R., 1981, *Prophecy and Praxis*.

Goulder, M.D., ed., 1968, *Infallibility in the Church*.

Gore, C., 1982, *The Mission of the Church*.

1900, *Roman Catholic Claims*.

1914, *The Basis of Anglican Fellowship in Faith and Organization*.

Haase, W., ed., 1982, *Rome and the Anglicans*. Berlin.

Hebblethwaite, P., 1980, *The New Inquisition? Schillebeeckx and Küng*.

Henson, H.H., 1939, *The Church of England*. Cambridge.

Hodges, H.A., 1979, *God Beyond Knowledge*.

Holland, H.S., 1908, *The Optimism of Butler's Analogy*. Oxford.

Hooker, R., 1845, *Of the Laws of Ecclesiastical Polity*, ed., J. Keble. Oxford.

Hort, F.J.A., 1894, *The Way, the Truth, the Life*.

Hügel, see von Hügel.

Hughes, J.J., 1971, 'Infallible? An Enquiry Considered' (*Theological Studies*, 32, pp. 183-207).

James, William, see Blanshard.

Khomyakov, A.S., 1977, 'On the Western Confessions of Faith', in A. Schmemann, ed., *Ultimate Questions: An Anthology of Modern Russian Religious Thought*. Oxford.

Koestler, A., 1964, *The Act of Creation*.

Küng, H., 1964, *The Council and Reunion*.

1965, *Structures of the Church*.

1971a, *Infallible?*

1971b, *The Church*.

1977, *On Being a Christian*.

1980, *The Church - Maintained in Truth*.

1981, *Justification*.

Lash, N., 1973, *Change in Focus*.

1981, *A Matter of Hope: A Theologian's Reflections on the Thought of Karl Marx*.

Locke, J., 1961, *Essay Concerning Human Understanding*. Everyman (Dent).

Loisy, A., see Reardon

Lonergan, B., 1957, *Insight*.

1972, *Method in Theology*.

1973, *Philosophy of God and Theology*.

Lossky, V., 1957, *The Mystical Theology of the Eastern Church*. Cambridge.

Luther, M., 1883—, *D. Martin Luthers Werke*, Weimarer Ausgabe. Weimar.

1955- *Luther's Works*. St Louis and Philadelphia.

'Lutherans and Catholics in Dialogue', 1974, V: *Papal Primacy and the Universal Church*. Minneapolis.

1980, VI: *Teaching Authority and Infallibility in the Church.* Minneapolis.

McAdoo, H.R., 1965. *The Spirit of Anglicanism.*

Macaulay, T.B., 1906, *History of England.*

Macmurray, J., 1957, *The Form of the Personal* : I. *The Self as Agent.*

1961, II. *Persons in Relation.*

Macquarrie, J., see Santer.

Mascall, E.L., 1977, *Theology and the Gospel of Christ.*

Maurice, F.D., 1835, *Subscription No Bondage.* Oxford.

1842, *Three Letters to the Rev. W. Palmer.*

1843, *Right and Wrong Methods of Supporting Protestantism.*

1872, *Moral and Metaphysical Philosophy.*

1904, 'On Words' (*The Friendship of Books*).

1958, *The Kingdom of Christ.*

Mendietta, see de Mendietta.

Meyendorff, J., 1966, *Orthodoxy and Catholicity*, New York.

Mill, J.S., 1950, *Mill on Bentham and Coleridge*, ed., F.R. Leavis.

More and Cross, eds., 1935, *Anglicanism.*

Naulty, R.A., 1973, 'Newman's Dispute with Locke' (*Journal of the History of Philosophy*, 11, pp. 453-7).

Neuner, J. and Dupuis, J., eds., 1983, *The Christian Faith in the Doctrinal Documents of the Catholic Church* (abbrev. DC).

Newman, J.H., 1841, *Tract 90.* Oxford.

1877, *The Prophetical Office of the Church.*

1903, *Essay in Aid of a Grammar of Assent.*

1915, *On University Education.*

1948, 'The Tamworth Reading Room' *Essays and Sketches*, II, ed., C.F. Harrold. New York.

1961, *On Consulting the Faithful in Matters of Doctrine*, ed., J. Coulson.

1970, *University Sermons.*

1974, *The Development of Christian Doctrine.* Penguin.

Owen, H.P., 1969, *The Christian Knowledge of God.*

Palmer, W., 1839, *Treatise on the Church of Christ.*

Pannenberg, W., 1970, *What is Man?* Philadelphia.

1976, *Theology and the Philosophy of Science.*

Pelikan, J., 1964, *Obedient Rebels.*

Plato, 1976 *Phaedrus and Letters VII and VIII.* Penguin.

Polanyi, M., 1958, *Personal Knowledge.*

1962, "The Unaccountable Element in Science" (*Philosophy*, 38, p. 11).

1967, *The Tacit Dimension.*

Popper, K., 1963, *Conjectures and Refutations.*

1972, *Objective Knowledge.* Oxford.

1976, *Unended Quest, An Intellectual Autobiography.*

Parker Society, 1840-, *The Works of the English Reformers*. Cambridge.

Rahner, K., 1965-, *Theological Investigations* (cited by vol. and page).

Ramsey, A.M., 1936, *The Gospel and the Catholic Church*.

    1945, 'What is Anglican Theology?' (*Theology*, 48, pp. 2-6).

    1951, *F.D. Maurice and the Conflicts of Modern Theology*. Cambridge.

Ratzinger, J., 1983, 'Anglican-Catholic Dialogue - Its Problems and Hopes', (*Insight*, 1, pp. 2-11).

Reardon, B.M.G., ed., 1970, *Roman Catholic Modernism*.

Santer, M., ed., 1982, *Their Lord and Ours*.

Satgé, J. de, 1981, *Peter and the Single Church*.

SCDF: Sacred Congregation for the Doctrine of the Faith, 1981, *Observations on the Final Report of ARCIC*.

Schillebeeckx, E., 1974, *The Understanding of Faith*.

Smith, J.E., 1968, *Experience and God*. New York.

Spens, W., 1917, *Belief and Practice*.

Stott, J., 1982, *Evangelical Anglicans and the ARCIC Final Report*. Bramcote, Notts.

Sykes, S.W., 1978, *The Integrity of Anglicanism*.

    1981, 'Authority in the Anglican Communion' (*Four Documents on Authority in the Anglican Communion*). Anglican Consultative Council.

    1982, 'ARCIC and the Papacy : An Examination of the Documents on Authority' (*The Modern Churchman*, 25, pp. 9-18).

    1984, *The Identity of Christianity*.

Tappert, T.G., ed., 1959, *The Book of Concord*. Philadelphia.

Taylor, A.E., 1951, *The Faith of a Moralist*.

Temple, W., 1934, *Nature, Man and God*.

    1958, *Religious Experience and Other Essays and Addresses*,

Thomas Aquinas, 1964-, *Summa Theologiae*. London and New York.

Thomas, P.H.E., 1982, 'The Lambeth Conferences and the Development of Anglican Ecclesiology, 1861-1978' (Ph.D. Thesis). Department of Theology, University of Durham.

Tillard, J., 1983, *The Bishop of Rome*.

Toynbee, P., 1982, *Towards the Holy Spirit*.

Tyrell, G., see Reardon.

Vatican II, Documents, see Abbott, W.M.

Vidler, A.R., 1957, *Essays in Liberality*.

von Balthasar, H.U., 1975, *Elucidations*.

von Hügel, F., 1921. 'Religion and Reality', in *Essays and Addresses on the Philosophy of Religion, I*.

Ware, T. 1964, *The Orthodox Church*. Penguin.

Warnock, M., 1976, *Imagination*.

Whitehead, A.N., 1926, *Religion in the Making*. Cambridge.

Bibliography

1938a, *Modes of Thought*. Cambridge.

1938b, *Science and the Modern World*. Penguin.

1941 *The Philosophy of A.N. Whitehead*, ed., P. Schilpp. Evanston and Chicago.

1942, *Adventures of Ideas*. Penguin.

1967, *Process and Reality*. New York.

Index of Subjects

Index of Names

141

DATE DUE